Inherited Wealth

INHERITED WEALTH
Opportunities and Dilemmas

by John L. Levy

CONTENTS

PREFACE

Few people understand the complexities of inherited wealth better than John Levy. Based on extensive personal experience, both with his own inherited wealth as well as guiding hundreds of dialogues with the wealthy families and their advisors, John's wise and caring words inspire us all. I say this with the perspective of more than twenty-five years of experience. I first met John Levy when I was in my early thirties and, as a young inheritor running a nonprofit called *Resourceful Women* (now called, *Inspired Legacies*), I was curious about whether he was genuinely empathetic or held stifling judgments about wealth holders. What I found in John was a quiet, yet bold and highly respected, sage who invited true dialogue and partnership. Over a number of years, we produced programs together and my own leadership was catapulted through his many introductions. By following John's gentle guidance and encouragement for trusting and exploring my own depth, I passed through a doorway of wealth and into the "richest" life of spirit and service. Since then, I have had the good fortune of leading thousands of other inheritors through this healing doorway.

The many insights presented here will long outlive John Levy. He offers a timeless understanding that is a gracious gift gleaned from a lifetime of listening to the diverse stories of persons of wealth. John's book shines with aliveness, truth telling, compassion and hope for inheritors, their families, and advisors. Here is a guidebook for the journey of awakening to the challenges and blessings of wealth. It is my hope that John's book will serve to unleash our generosity—for ourselves, those we know, and those in greatest need—for healing ourselves and the planet that John has graced, and loves so much.

Tracy Gary
Inspired Legacies

FOREWORD

I have been using John Levy's wisdom and insight in my financial planning practice in working with affluent families since I first met John about 10 years ago. His work has impacted my practice of financial planning profoundly. John introduced me to a framework for simplifying the often complex interactions between the creators of wealth and inheritors. Here we have insights and wisdom in an area seldom explored: the issues of wealth complicated by the intricacies of the human psyche and family systems.

With this book, John's original articles are now updated and presented as a cohesive whole. You will find writings that explain with clarity, matters of which most families have a visceral awareness but cannot often articulate. The intricacies of our situations can be so subtle that we frequently cannot put our finger on the core issues, yet John lays them out in ways that are intuitive; leading us to experience a connection with what we already knew at a deep level.

After recognizing what we previously knew, John inspires us with a vision of an enriched life that "includes personal and spiritual growth, contribution, and legacy" that flows out of our deepest and most important values. We are equipped to engage in an authentic process addressing solutions to our own unique challenges.

When we deal with our professional advisors in financial matters, the advice we often receive can be focused on the advisor's area of expertise, be technically correct, yet miss the mark of what individuals and families most need. John puts financial, estate and tax advice in the context of individual and family needs so that it serves and strengthens family relationships. We are shown principles that empower and not weaken loved ones for whom our resources can impact in profound ways.

As we read, we can see how the wisdom of this book was developed from a long career of advising wealthy families. We see past common solutions and begin to see a vision of wealth beyond financial resources yet enriched by them—true wealth.

May you engage in a process of using the intelligence found herein so your wealth provides you with significant meaning, utmost utility and makes a contribution.

J. Jeffrey Lambert, CFP®
Lighthouse Financial Planning, LLC
Sacramento, CA

ACKNOWLEDGMENTS

I wish to express my great appreciation to all the people who have helped me to learn and to grow in this profession. These include, especially, my clients, who have honored me with their trust and have taught me so much, by their words and their examples, about wealth, its uses, and the process of transmission.

I've also been privileged to work and to be with many financial professionals—in conferences, in personal meetings, and in their articles and books—who have shared their experience and their wisdom.

Andy Reed has my gratitude for proposing that my writings be turned into a book and getting the project underway.

My dear friends, Duane and Coleen Elgin, have contributed so much to this book and to my life. Coleen has been tireless and brilliant in bringing the book to fruition, in creating my website (johnllevy.com), and being helpful and supportive in so many ways. Duane has done superb editing to make the articles more readable and coherent.

I very much appreciate the generous Preface and Foreword from Tracy Gary and Jeff Lambert, two highly regarded professionals in the worlds of philanthropy and financial planning. Their comments made me even happier to have this book available.

My thanks also to several of my friends who have been most helpful in reading and improving the articles as they developed.

Most of all, I want to dedicate this book to my beloved wife, Adele Schwarz, for her continuing support of me and my work.

INTRODUCTION

This book is intended for wealthy parents, their children, and the professionals who serve them. It may also be of interest to anyone who wants to learn about the issues of inherited wealth. The book is based on articles that I have written over the past twenty-five years as part of my professional life—working with affluent individuals and families on personal issues that arise in relation to wealth and, especially, the transmission of wealth through inheritance. I include discussions of the challenges and dilemmas that often accompany inheriting wealth and suggestions for how these can be resolved. I also explore the potential for an enriched life for those inheriting wealth—one that includes personal and spiritual growth, contribution, and legacy.

My work, reflected in this book, has the overarching purpose of assisting affluent individuals and families to regard and use their wealth in ways that enrich their own lives and those of others with whom they are connected. An underlying purpose is to suggest that wealthy people use their money and power to benefit others and our world.

I hope that those of you who read this will find it helpful in your own lives.

John L. Levy
Mill Valley, California
March 2008

CHAPTER 1
Coping with Inherited Wealth: An Overview

There are many reasons to build and maintain a personal fortune. But suppose one's wealth is adequate to assure a high standard of living for the rest of life? Then the question arises: Why keep amassing more money, particularly if this requires a good deal of effort and interferes with enjoyment of the fortune they've acquired? One of the more common reasons—and one that is socially sanctioned—is to provide opportunities, comfort, and security for their children and their children's children. Obviously this is a fine and a worthy thing to do. What caring parent doesn't want his or her children to be secure, comfortable, and to have all of the opportunities and rewards that affluence can bring?

However, a growing number of parents as well as inheritors are increasingly questioning the assumption that inheriting wealth results in happier, more fulfilling and more productive lives. A substantial amount of evidence reveals that receiving wealth doesn't always work out that way. Many people who grew up in affluence, knowing that they could expect to receive without effort all that they needed and perhaps considerably more, have found that this hasn't been an unmitigated blessing. Too often they are not very happy or fulfilled. Sometimes they are depressed, anxious, lost, and dispirited.

The noted Swiss psychiatrist, Carl Jung, counseled a rich young person in this way: "You have acquired a false security, and it is this false security on which you live that causes your feeling of inferiority. One lives wrapped in cotton, protected from the cold and the heat. It is not good never to be cold or hot." He then went on to tell this story about one of his clients: "A famous composer had a friend, a patron, who had given him a beautiful villa and had guaranteed him an income and an opulent life. The composer composed nothing anymore. After some time he comes to see me. 'I am obsessed by a dream: I have received a mortal wound, I bleed profusely and nothing can stop the hemorrhage.' I counsel him: 'You have become too rich, give a part away.' Violent denials. Some time later the patron stops a part of his contributions. A great shock for the composer. Six months later he had composed a very good opera."

I am not suggesting that inheriting money is always an unfortunate experience and that the kindest thing that wealthy parents could do for their children is to cut them off with little or no inheritance. The good news is that some people who receive substantial wealth from their families do very well with it and lead happy, creative, and satisfying lives. It is both interesting and useful to look at the successful examples—to learn what their parents have done, what other circumstances have operated, and what the children have done for themselves.

With these sorts of questions in mind, I engaged in a five-year study, inspired and funded by a wealthy man who was concerned about the effects of inherited wealth on his own children as well as others. While the project was aimed at identifying and understanding of some of the problems, which can accompany substantial inheritance, its primary purpose was to seek ways in which these difficulties can be eliminated or ameliorated.

In the course of this study I interviewed some thirty wealthy parents and inheritors, counseled some of them, perused the available literature (which was surprisingly scant), and participated in the supervision of two doctoral dissertations on inheritance issues. In addition I interviewed and talked with a considerable number of psychotherapists about the special problems that inheritor clients bring to them and their insights as to how these problems can best be avoided or dealt with. I also brought my own background to this study, having grown up in moderate affluence and in a community largely populated by the truly wealthy. Since completing the study I have been a consultant to wealthy individuals and families on these issues, and this book also reflects what I have learned in my consulting practice.

A MODEL OF PSYCHOLOGICAL DEVELOPMENT

In looking at the difficulties that often afflict young inheritors, it is useful to keep in mind the psychological development of a person and the stages of growing into a reasonably whole human being. Erik Erikson was a highly respected psychoanalyst and authority on the process of human development. He concluded that certain tasks need to be confronted in the course of maturation. Each is experienced as a crisis that, if resolved, leads to healthy development; if not, then the person is, to some extent, psychologically damaged. Many persons are unable to deal with these challenges when they first come up, but do manage them, to an extent at least, later in life. But some don't.

In his *Growth and Crises of the Healthy Personality*, Erikson proposes the following tasks need to be completed by the developing person, more or less in the order that they ordinarily arise. For each he also describes the consequences of failure to meet the particular challenge. I shall mention each of these briefly to provide a framework for understanding what can happen in the development of the inheritor.

The first challenge that Erikson describes is developing an attitude of **Basic Trust**. This is defined as "...reasonable trustfulness as far as others are concerned and a simple sense of trustworthiness as far as oneself is concerned." Failure to achieve basic trust results in an attitude of mistrust.

The next challenge is to achieve **Autonomy** or "...a sense of rightful dignity and lawful independence." Failure to experience this sense of autonomy leads to shame and doubt, a feeling of being "...completely exposed and conscious of being looked at..."

The succeeding crucial task is to feel able to take **Initiative**, "...to be self-activated...in the free possession of a certain surplus of energy that permits him to forget failures quickly and to approach what seems desirable (even if it also seems dangerous) with undiminished and better aimed effort." Not achieving a sense of initiative leads to pervasive feelings of guilt.

The next life crisis unfolds around **Industry** or the ability to learn and to accomplish. This has both a solitary aspect—to be able to achieve by oneself—and a communal aspect—to be able to work, and to play, with others. When not experienced, the outcome is often a sense of being inferior.

The last of Erikson's developmental stages requires meeting the preceding challenges fairly well and is that of acquiring a clear sense of our **Identity**. Simply stated, this is knowing who we are and being reasonably comfortable with this awareness. It means that we neither feel the need to conform to the expectations of others or to rebel against them.

PROBLEMS THAT OFTEN ACCOMPANY INHERITANCE

Building upon Erikson's insights, below are my observations on the challenges that often accompany substantial inheritance. I describe important problems that often accompany inheritance, reasons why these problems are likely to occur, and helpful suggestions for both parents and inheritors.

Self-esteem is often diminished

Often, children of wealth are unable to fully value or to admire themselves, and this results in considerable suffering. This is not surprising, since the experience of gaining inherited wealth can interfere with mastering Erikson's developmental tasks that are essential for true self-esteem.

Achieving what Erikson calls "Autonomy" is particularly crucial for a sense of personal adequacy. It is often difficult for inheritors to value their accomplishments or to take much satisfaction in them since they suspect their successes are partly the result of their inherited wealth and position. Instead of feeling autonomous, many feel a lack of confidence that they could achieve anything significant or that they would be liked and respected by others if they were not affluent. These self-doubts are often reinforced by the behavior of others who resent the good fortune of the inheritor.

One form of low self-esteem that is found especially among some inheritors is the fear of failure that is related to difficulties in meeting the tasks that Erikson called "Initiative" and "Industry." This is especially true in the area of vocation. If a person has never had to earn their living they don't really know that they could. Often this fear prevents individuals from taking the initiative and the risks required for vocational achievements. Understandably, self-doubt is often exacerbated when their parents have been notably successful in their lives and work.

Inheritors are often delayed in their emotional development.

A substantial inheritance often results in delayed maturation. Like the butterfly that never develops adequately if it gets external help breaking out of its cocoon, many inheritors are spared important life challenges. The crises and challenges that Erikson postulates as necessary for healthy development of the personality can be avoided, diminished or delayed by the person who is protected by the comfort and security that money provides. As Jung describes, they are "wrapped in cotton." Just as body-builders and athletes say "no pain, no gain," intellectual and emotional development seems also to require effort in overcoming challenges and ordeals. Protecting the inheritor from life's traumas and stresses not only inhibits development, it can also serve to dampen the whole quality of their life experience. In limiting pain we almost inevitably cut off some of the delight at the other end of the spectrum. I am not suggesting that rich and over-protected children never grow up, but often they do so more slowly than those whose lives are more difficult and stressful. Most of us don't mature any faster than we absolutely must and inheritors are more able than most to avoid or delay the process.

Inheritors often lack strong motivation.

Lack of incentive is both the cause and the result of failure to meet adequately the challenges that Erikson calls "Industry" and "Initiative." This can be a particular problem in choosing and following careers. A large inheritance can make it difficult to sustain an interest in and a commitment to anything that requires intense and continuing effort and the endurance of ambiguity, setbacks, and frustration. Often the goals of inheritors—in work and in other aspects of their lives—are not well defined or strongly desired, and this makes it difficult to mobilize their efforts to pursue these goals. This is particularly true when goals are set by their parents and aren't truly those of the inheritor. Certainly there are notable exceptions to this but inheritance may also be a challenge for many who are driven by a need to prove that they are not just lucky inheritors. Despite such exceptions, the motivational drive of those who inherit wealth is often short-lived and/or not very intense.

Inheritors may have difficulty with self-discipline.

Inheritors often find great difficulty in focusing their energy on pursuits that have meaning for them, and then sticking with these long enough to obtain truly satisfying outcomes. Self-discipline requires concentration and focused energy, as well as the ability to postpone gratification in the interest of rewards that are ultimately more satisfying. These qualities often seem incompatible with the silver spoon—which suggests immediate feeding. Self-discipline is necessary not only for work, but also for significant relationships and life-enhancing experiences such as psychotherapy and the quest for spiritual development.

Many inheritors are bored by their lives.

Boredom isn't surprising as a rich, young person's existence and activities often don't seem very real or very intense. Nothing matters that much. Lack of commitment leads to waning interest, which often results in carelessness and irresponsibility in work and in relationships. The results (or lack of results) of such behavior ultimately turn back and intensify the boredom. Ennui is one of the more painful consequences of failure to meet the developmental challenges as they arise. In turn, boredom often leads to misuse of alcohol and other drugs, and to self-destructive behavior.

Inheritors often have difficulty in the use of power.

One of the principal ingredients of a life that is lived well is the appropriate and effective use of one's power, both situational and personal. This is related to Erikson's belief that people must learn to take initiative and to express industriousness. Power presents a particular peril to inheritors since they haven't earned it themselves and often don't feel entitled to it.

The special world in which inheritors grow up can be insulated from the competitive arenas in which power is normally exercised. They often have problems, not only with the power that comes to them by virtue of their wealth and position, but also with the personal power within themselves. Inheritors may be extreme in the ways they handle power: avoiding it and denying its reality, or exercising it arbitrarily and self-servingly, riding roughshod over people as an over-compensation for their sense of inadequacy and confusion. Either course can make it hard to work and live with others.

Inheritors often suffer from guilt.

One of the best-known prices that many pay for inheriting wealth is guilt. They find it hard to accept unmerited good fortune and may not be able to find ways to prove themselves worthy of it. When a person has not played much of a part in creating their favored place in the world, it is hard not to keep wondering, "Why me?" The kind of maturation that is developed in meeting the task of "Autonomy"—knowing who one is—can ameliorate this sense of guilt and make it both more conscious and more tolerable. Still, it may not be possible for the inheritors of substantial wealth to escape some of the burden of feeling guilty. Such guilt can be experienced and expressed in ways ranging from feeling abjectly apologetic for their good fortune to being arrogantly contemptuous.

Inheritors often experience alienation

Wealthy people generally, and inheritors especially, are often afflicted by feelings of separation. Many of the rich feel different from other people. Particularly if they were born into affluence, they find it hard to understand the lives and experience of those in more ordinary circumstances, and they are equally convinced (with some validity) that the others can't understand theirs. They may choose to associate almost entirely with their economic peers. But it's still difficult to escape the sense of being alienated and different from most people.

Inheritors are often suspicious

Erikson pointed out the crucial importance of developing a sense of trust as the first of the developmental tasks and one that is a prerequisite to all the others. But the rich tend to see other people as not to be trusted, often for quite good reasons. Many of those they encounter want something from the affluent person and are ready to manipulate or use him or her for their own purposes. Wealthy people sense that many who are less well off resent their favored status, particularly if it is inherited, and this resentment often takes the form of thinly disguised anger. All these reasons can add up to one of the most painful and damaging aspects of inheritance—difficulty in believing that people like and appreciate them just for themselves. Mistrust often gets in the way of developing true friends and living and working companions.

Men and women inheritors face different problems

While many of the difficulties that confront inheritors are likely to be common to both females and males, some are not. Generally, young men are more apt to have trouble with career choices and achievements, while young women have even more difficulty than men (or non-wealthy women) in establishing their credibility and competence. A woman who puts on seminars for women who have inherited, or expect to inherit, substantial wealth says: "Women face unique problems with inherited wealth that has mostly to do with their being left out of the decision-making process. The older men and the brothers in the family have traditionally been given that responsibility. Men have tended to be much more involved in the family business than women. We're sort of kept in this 'You needn't worry about this, dear,' posture.

SOURCES OF THESE PROBLEMS

If there's nothing intrinsically wrong with wealth, even if it is inherited, then why do so many inheritors exhibit these painful and unfortunate symptoms? There are a number of reasons for this and some of them are within the power of the wealthy to do something about and some are not.

The affluent encounter negativity from others

Among those causes that can't be helped are the attitudes that the affluent run up against in those who are less fortunate. As we have seen, these include envy, anger, and resentment and often an objectionable obsequiousness. Many middle-income people find it difficult to behave normally in the presence of those they regard as "rich." Also, inheritors have difficulty getting a sympathetic hearing for their troubles. Most Americans seem to believe that if they only had enough money and the things it can buy, then they would live in a state of constant bliss. Consequently they tend to respond disdainfully to any indication of suffering by the affluent, particularly if these are people who didn't earn their fortunes. When I talk about my work, I often hear less affluent persons say, "I wish I had those kinds of problems." And it's clear that the media delight in reporting the tribulations and foolishness of the rich.

Our cultural values often make life difficult for the inheritor

Another source of difficulty is that many have absorbed the Judeo-Christian-capitalist tradition that places great value on self-reliance and earning one's own way. These values can oppress the inheritor in more or less subtle ways. Also in this heritage is the value of egalitarianism and the assumption that everyone should have equal opportunity—politically, in the exercise of power; economically, in the possibility of rising in the world; and psycho-spiritually, in opportunities for personal development. The inheritance of affluence is quite contrary to this and is a painful reminder that, as a culture, we do not live what we profess.

Too many options can cause problems.

Another difficulty that often afflicts inheritors is the availability of too many choices in life. We assume that we want as many options as we can have, because one of the curses of poverty is limited opportunity. But many persons cannot cope well with having so many possibilities and choices. A plenitude of options can be paralyzing and can make it very difficult to develop the capacity to make sensible and intelligent decisions.

It is hard to be sure you could live without your inherited wealth.

An underlying and rarely conscious cause of the problems that can beset inheritors is the fear of losing their wealth. If we have never had to support ourselves, never had to make our way in the world without the security of a sizeable fortune, then it's hard to be confident that we could do so if this became necessary. This produces a gnawing fear of what might happen if the money were to somehow disappear. No matter how irrational this might seem, the underlying feeling can be what's been called "the bag-lady syndrome"—a sense of panic that, "If I lost my money I could never survive. I'd die." Surprisingly to those who are not wealthy, this can even afflict inheritors who have substantial fortunes.

A related problem is fear of failure. One may not grapple with challenges if they feel unsure they have what it takes to surmount them. A failure to develop what Erikson calls "industry" can be especially painful and limiting for the young persons whose parents were exceptionally successful and for those who grow up under the burden of excessive parental expectations. Being viewed as "rich" can interfere with personal development and creativity.

Even when the wealthy have developed themselves with talent, competence, and taste, they still must overcome pressures to substitute money for their own services. These pressures are both from within (it's easier to write a check than to do hard work) and from without (people often seem to want their money more than their talents and energy). For example, when the wealthy involve themselves in charity and cause work, they're usually expected to provide and to raise funds, and this often interferes with recognition of their personal abilities.

Inheritors often don't receive good parenting.

It is unfortunately true that many wealthy parents are neglectful of their children. Because they tend to lead busy and active lives, they may wish to spare themselves the stress and messiness of bringing up young ones. I've heard so many sad descriptions of growing up with parents who substituted material gifts for love and attention.

Also, affluent parents are able to purchase childcare from servants and boarding schools. The servants and the schools may be fine in many ways but they are still surrogates and they cannot provide the kind of personal attention and caring that are so needed and wanted from parents. When parental care and love are faulty or inadequate, it's hard for the child to deal with the first of the tasks of maturing—learning to be trusting.

A related difficulty is that some rich parents are too intrusive in the lives of their children. Parental concern for the family fortune can result in excessive interference in their children's lives and this not only diminishes trust but also keeps the children from maturing properly.

It is hard to be part of a dynasty.

Particularly in families with an established tradition of wealth and position, high parental expectations are a major force. Many such families raise their children, generation after generation, with considerable pressure to achieve and maintain very high standards of excellence—personally, socially and vocationally—and to maintain and grow the family fortune. While this can operate quite constructively for some inheritors, for others it can be very burdensome, even counter-productive. This is particularly true when the same standards are applied to all the children, regardless of their individual capabilities and interests. A particular struggle for inheritors is establishing their own individual identity, rather than being seen primarily as members of a wealthy family.

Considering these perils and pitfalls can seem quite discouraging to wealthy parents and their children. It is not hard to understand why thoughtful, wealthy parents may believe that their fortune could best be bequeathed to worthy charitable causes, saving their children from the kind of misery and stress that inheritance often brings. Some very well known people of wealth have made such decisions, giving their children a good education and then turning them loose with little or no inheritance to find their own way in the world. However, I see such decisions as being quite unfortunate.

From my own experience, and that of many I've known, inheriting a substantial amount can be a truly wonderful blessing, not a curse. It provides the inheritor opportunities to choose among career options, some of which may not be income producing. Being able to select a vocation in philanthropy, social service, teaching or the arts is a wonderful privilege that wise parents can offer their children.

We all know or know of inheritors who seem to have made it, who have not only survived that experience without visible scars but have even used their good fortune to enhance their own lives and to contribute to the world around them. What accounts for their benefiting from their inheritance, when some don't? The suggestions that follow are based on observations of individuals and families where the inheritance process seemed to be handled well.

SUGGESTIONS TO WEALTHY PARENTS AND THEIR CHILDREN

It is important for parents to be thoughtful about how much to leave their children as well as when and how they leave it. A range of alternatives exist regarding how much should be available to the children and when they should have access to it. Many wealthy parents have decided that the young people will have to support themselves, at least partially, if they want to live in the style to which they have become accustomed. Others choose to make capital, as well as income, available quite early in life. An important caution here is that when parents make these decisions, it's important that the children know what is going to happen and that they understand the reasons for it. As one wealthy parent put it: "It's not right to bring them up on steak and then make them switch to hamburger."

Good child rearing is especially important for inheritors.

Thoughtful and caring parenting provides the kind of love, training, counsel, and examples that support development through the various stages of childhood and adolescence. It is particularly important that both parents provide quality time for the children and serve as good listeners, really trying to hear what their children are saying to them. Wise and loving nurturing are crucial for those who grow up with the paradoxical problems that can accompany the anticipation of a lifetime of security and comfort.

A particularly important task for the affluent parent is to teach children to endure the frustration of delays and disappointments and to resist the temptation to quit when things aren't going their way. Setting good examples is vastly more effective than simply telling young people how to behave. "Do as I say, not as I do," may be appealing to parents but it is not effective as teaching.

The pitfalls of bringing up children in wealth, and with the anticipation of being affluent, are sufficiently thorny and subtle that many parents will be well advised to seek professional help. For some this will mean psychotherapy for the parents and professional help for the children. Others will choose to seek the guidance of someone who specializes in the difficulties that can afflict inheritors.

Parental surrogates can play significant roles.

Inheritors often talk of servants providing a crucial role in their growth.

While wise parents will avoid the danger of delegating too much of the responsibilities of child rearing to employees, they must recognize how much influence these people have in the development of their children. Servants are usually peripheral to the lives of the parents but children, who are more restricted in their life space, experience them as important and highly valued relationships. People who grew up with servants often speak of the deep pain they suffered when retainers who had been important figures in their lives suddenly disappeared, either by dismissal or resignation. Unfortunately this often happens without adequate or even truthful explanations to the children, leaving them puzzled and pained.

It is important for parents to give serious consideration to the selection of servants and to use care in observing and evaluating them in their relationships with the children. Many people have reported experiences of cruelty and neglect by servants that were simply not noticed or taken seriously by their parents. Also, the ways in which parents treat servants inevitably guides their children, for better or for worse, in their future relationships with employees and with non-affluent people.

Young people often have important relationships with other adults who serve somewhat as parental figures for them. These include teachers, counselors, scoutmasters, athletic coaches, family friends and others. Wise parents will encourage the formation of such relationships between their children and those adult surrogates who have a beneficial influence on them. Although they will do what they can to discourage those connections that do not seem helpful to the children, they will need to be careful that they don't disapprove of such relationships simply because they involve people of different backgrounds and values.

Inheritors must be taught sound attitudes toward their affluence.

It is important for wealthy parents to teach their children constructive ways of living with their wealth. This starts with the parents themselves being relatively comfortable, clear, and balanced about their own wealth, free of both pride and shame about it. Parents need to start with a good look at themselves, searching out their own attitudes toward affluence and what comes with it, and then working through whatever they find that is unresolved, as best they can, in order to avoid contaminating their children. Parents need to demonstrate healthy and appropriate ways of using money wisely, avoiding the extremes of profligacy and penury. The manner in which parents manage their own money inevitably serves to teach their children about ethical and psychological values far more than what the parents tell them.

One factor that seems to distinguish those who function well with inherited wealth is that their parents have dealt with them openly and straightforwardly about money. As with sex, children's real questions about the family fortune and their own prospects should be responded to directly. In my research and consulting, I found it remarkable how few inheritors felt their parents really did this for them. If the wealth and its eventual transmission to the children are dealt with covertly by the parents—as so many parents used to avoid the topic of sex—children are apt to see the money as something dark and shameful. This makes it less likely that they will be comfortable with themselves as inheritors.

Also, if their parents won't talk with them about this topic, children will take this to mean they aren't trusted, which may lower their self-esteem. This doesn't mean instructing toddlers about financial statements, but it does suggest being attentive to children's questions and sensitive to their growing ability to deal with such matters.

Parents are often uneasy about dealing with their young children's questions about financial matters (e.g. "How much money have we?" "How much does Daddy make?") I find that using these questions as an occasion for conversation can prove richly rewarding. Parents may want first to explore with the child what the real question is. It may be a search for security: "Are we going to be all right?"

When parents decide a child isn't ready to be told about certain matters, it's important that they let her or him know that the information will be forthcoming at some reasonably specified time in the future. Most importantly, children should never be made to feel that any question is bad or illegitimate and that there's something wrong with them for asking it. As they mature the children are likely to want to know more and more about the family fortunes:

Where did the money come from (including whether it's from the father's or mother's side and which generation made it)?

How large is the fortune?

How much, when and under what conditions (trusts, etc.) can they reasonably expect to receive for themselves?

Children also need instruction, both verbally and by example, as to how money is to be used. Parents should keep their growing children aware of some of the pitfalls and problems associated with wealth, particularly by drawing their attention to individuals and families who are handling their money and position, either especially well or quite badly. As they become more able and interested, children should participate in discussions of the kinds of obligations and ethical issues that accompany affluence so that they can see their fortunes as carrying certain responsibilities to the society in which they live.

It is valuable to familiarize children with the use of money when they are quite young, starting with such things as allowances. An allowance should be seen as the child's right, not as a reward for good behavior, subject to being withheld as punishment. Nor should the child's allowance require the performance of chores. Sharing in the work of maintaining the household should be established as a condition of being a member of that household and not reimbursed by money. On the other hand, it is often helpful to pay children to perform tasks beyond what is expected of them as family members.

As they grow older, children can learn by experience about budgeting their expenses, handling their checking accounts, dealing with credit cards, and the consequences of fiscal irresponsibility. Paid summer jobs are almost always a good idea, for a number of reasons, including helping the children to believe that they really can support themselves. Ideally the children should find their own jobs, without help from their parents.

Rich children particularly want a sense of their heritage.

All children, and especially the wealthy, benefit from a sense of family pride, and instilling this is another parental responsibility. Wherever the money originally came from, the children want to feel good about it and about the people who made it, managed it, and in whose line they are. What's important is that they grow up feeling that they have a background of which they can be proud and that there are admirable traditions to uphold. In those situations where the fortune was made in ways that are difficult to justify, I can only suggest candor and a clear commitment on the part of the parents to use their affluence in socially responsible ways.

Choosing schools involves important and thorny decisions.

It is difficult to generalize since the right choice is a very individual matter and depends on a number of factors, including the nature of the family and the particular qualities of the child. The big decisions are public versus private and, if the latter, day schools vs. boarding schools. The advantages and disadvantages of each, in terms of intellectual as well as psychological, emotional, and social development, are too complex to go into here. These are not easy choices. For one child a private boarding school, some distance from home, may be the right choice at a particular point while going to a local public school may well be appropriate at some other point. Employing an educational consultant to provide information about schools and to help in the decisions is often a wise move.

One temptation for parents to avoid is to pressure the children to enroll in schools that one of their parents attended. Also, if a boarding school is chosen, it's essential that this be discussed so that the child is not left with the feeling that the parents are just getting rid of him or her.

Involving the children in these decisions, particularly as they grow older, is always a good idea. It is important that they participate in the considerations that led up to the decision, and that their points of view and feelings were heard and respected (although not necessarily followed). Being active participants in decisions that affect their lives can be very helpful in alleviating some of the problems that can accompany being a passive inheritor.

The transmission of wealth is a complex and individual issue.

At one level this is a matter of practical economics: minimizing income and inheritance taxes, preserving capital through sound investing, and safeguarding the fortune against such contingencies as bad marriages, foolish investments, extravagant spending, and unwise loans or gifts by the children. There are tricky ethical and psychological issues involved and the decisions that are made as to how the money is to be preserved and transmitted have important effects on the children's attitudes toward their parents, their feelings about themselves, and their ability to deal with their fortunes as they gain control over them.

Wills and trusts are a complex and perilous territory. The tax laws are now so arcane and complex that an attorney who specializes in such matters should craft anything beyond the simplest estate plan. It is important that children be kept informed from childhood and that their wishes and concerns be heard and considered. The importance of this two-way communication can hardly be overestimated. I have been pained and shocked to discover how rare it is for parents to be open with their heirs in dealing with this topic. I often encourage day-long meetings of the parents with those children old enough to participate meaningfully. When tensions are rather high or conflict is anticipated, it can be most helpful to use the services of a skilled and neutral facilitator. Often children learn about the amounts and conditions of their inheritances only after their parents' death, and this is generally detrimental to their personal well being as well as their ability to manage their fortunes responsibly. Surprises in this circumstance are never a good idea.

It is generally very helpful to heirs to be given control over some significant portion of their inheritances at reasonably early ages. Being kept on an allowance serves not only to inhibit development, it also conveys a clear message that they are not trusted.

One system for transmitting an inheritance that has been used successfully by some wealthy parents is to make some fraction (perhaps one-third) of their inheritance available to their children at a rather young age, say twenty-one, with the understanding that a second third will be turned over to them after they've demonstrated some ability to use it responsibly, and then the final third held back until it's quite clear, to the parents and/or trustees, that the inheritor is mature enough to take responsibility for it. This also minimizes the likelihood of their losing too much of their inheritance through foolishness or naiveté.

Parents sometimes use the promise of inheritance as a means of coercing the children to behave "appropriately". While tempting, this sort of manipulation is a danger to be avoided; it's almost always destructive. While it's true that inheritance should depend on some demonstration of ability to handle the money responsibly, there is danger in the use of this kind of power to force the child to dissemble and to deny his or her true nature.

Another obvious caution is that the parents' distribution of their wealth among their children must be fair to all. This doesn't necessarily mean that they are treated equally, but when the distribution isn't equal, it's important that they all understand the reasons for the differences and can accept this without undue resentment.

Sound career choices are crucial and difficult for inheritors.

Following in parent's footsteps is often a mistake, particularly when they have been exceptionally successful. If the young person tries to compete with a parent, it's likely to be a painfully losing proposition. It is hard to maintain intensity of motivation and interest when bringing in more money feels meaningless and not of benefit to anyone. For such children, choosing a vocation in the arts, sciences, philanthropy or the academic world may offer an attractive and satisfying answer. Success and achievement in these fields are less likely to be seen by others as well as themselves as unmerited and due to the family fortune and status.

In seeking a career that can be both challenging and rewarding, many affluent people have found satisfaction in fields that transcend the world of the material such as philanthropy or public service. Such vocations can fill lives with meaning and excitement, providing wonderful opportunities for creativity. Andrew Carnegie discovered that it was easier to make money than to give it away wisely. Inheritors can serve actively in family or other charitable trusts, and they can involve themselves as board members or volunteers for various service, advocacy, and charitable organizations.

In seeking a career that can be both challenging and rewarding, many affluent people have entered the realm of the aesthetic. The wealthy have unique opportunities to relate to the artistic world—as creators, as patrons, as collectors, or simply as appreciators. In a world that seems to be growing increasingly tasteless and ugly, such a career can offer special opportunities for satisfying work, particularly for people who can bring to it not only their affluence but also rich cultural backgrounds and knowledge.

It is important for young, affluent persons to find work in which they are not identified as different, and where they have opportunities to prove themselves simply on the basis of who they are and what they do. In short, it is important for them to succeed on their own merits.

In order to attain a sense of success and competence in the world of work, the inheritor must be willing to stay in the situation long enough to have a chance to surmount the obstacles and setbacks that are bound to occur. This means fighting against the tendency of many inheritors to resign or make other shifts when the level of frustration and discouragement becomes very high. One of the differences between those who made fortunes and those who inherited them is just this—the builders have both the willingness and the ability to hang in when the going gets tough. Inheritors often haven't had much experience of slogging through difficult and frustrating times, and it's hard for them to recognize the value of enduring such pain when it can be avoided.

Successful inheritors work at their own personal development.

Psychological and spiritual growth are essential for everyone but is particularly important for the affluent because of their need to find meaning in their lives beyond the materialistic and competitive realms. Also, they are likely to have more leisure to ponder, to be concerned about, and perhaps to do something about these aspects of their lives. Wise parents will provide guidance here, as well as seeing that their children have opportunities to develop in these ways. Parents can assist their children growing up without a sense of stigma regarding psychotherapy. They can encourage them and give them opportunities to explore different forms of psychotherapy. Neither therapy nor particular therapists should be imposed on the children but they can be encouraged to seek their own when it seems to fit for them. A number of the inheritors with whom I have met have testified to the importance of these experiences in their lives.

It is important that both parents and children view psychotherapy, not as the treatment of illness, but as a life-enhancing experience, a significant element in their education for living. It is important to emphasize how valuable a wise, skilled and understanding psychotherapist can be. Good therapy can be profoundly useful in helping young people find their own answers to existential questions they must answer if their lives are to have meaning. Therapy can be of great help as inheritors struggle with the special problems that confront them.

One challenge to be watched is the tendency of some inheritors to view their therapist as a servant. When the experience becomes difficult and unpleasant (as it will) they may choose to terminate it ("fire the therapist"). Also, it is important to find a therapist who is neither awed nor antagonized by their wealth.

I also recommend similar attitudes for spiritual development and practices. For some this could mean a conventional church-oriented religion and for others a more individual way. As with psychotherapy and its ramifications, parents teach partly by example and partly by encouragement and by making opportunities available. All of us find life more fulfilling if we have at least some sense of reality and significance beyond that which is just physical and rational, and this is particularly true for the rich who usually find that material abundance just isn't enough for a satisfying life.

Relationships are a crucial element in a good life

Friends and associates who are not resentful or envious and who do not wish to exploit the relationship can be very helpful in coping with the challenges of wealth. These may be people who have enough money themselves or who, while not especially well off financially, have lives sufficiently full that they can relate to the affluent person simply and directly, without flattery or manipulation, and free of resentment or envy.

Inheritors need to know they can function without their money.

My observations show that those inheritors who seem least damaged by their good fortune are the ones who have proven to themselves that they are competent, worthwhile, and don't need the family money to lead successful lives. These are people who have dealt successfully with the developmental challenges that Erikson describes, who have achieved Basic Trust, developed their sense of Autonomy, learned to take Initiative, developed a capacity for Industry, and come to a sense of their own Identity.

To achieve all this, rich young people need to have some experience at earning a living so they can feel confident that they can support themselves and not be dependent on inherited wealth. Parents need to encourage this, and actively help their children learn to support themselves and to feel confident in their ability to do so. Such self-confidence can only come from experience.

An attitude of stewardship is of great value to the inheritor.

Children of affluence should be taught about charitable giving from an early age, verbally as well as by the examples of their parents. In my discussions with inheritors, as well as in the research I've done, it has been striking to observe the correlation between an attitude of using wealth in socially responsible ways and having a sense of comfort and satisfaction with being affluent. In addition to philanthropy, investing their funds in companies that they see making positive contributions to society can be very rewarding to the inheritor as well as to our world.

One wealthy young woman wrote me: "Between some positive family influence and encountering new channels for handling/utilizing money, I've been feeling better about it all the time. Most recently I've been working with a financial planner who specializes in 'Socially Responsible Investing', which makes the 'burden' of wealth quite palatable, even fun."

Giving or investing to benefit society can provide inheritors with a sense of meaning and purpose and help them to realize that they are valuable and worthwhile members of society. It can also offer areas of learning and involvement that keep them interested and excited, as well as providing the kind of joy—cited by all of the great spiritual teachers and guides—that accompanies the act of giving.

Inheritors need to take risks with people.

A certain amount of suspiciousness is certainly realistic and appropriate for the wealthy, but when it is too pervasive and excessive it limits their lives severely. They will usually find it worthwhile to risk making favorable assumptions about love partners, friends and associates and entering into true commitments in these relationships. While such risks will expose them to the possibility of being hurt, they can open opportunities for full and rewarding relationships. Erikson postulates *trust* as the primary achievement necessary for psychological maturation, and here is one aspect of life where it can be nurtured and tested. Sometimes this will result in disappointment, disillusionment and pain, but the rewards can be sufficient to make the risks worth taking. And it's almost the only way really to learn to tell which people can be trusted. Here again parental examples of willingness to risk appropriately can be most helpful.

Many inheritors will be parents of inheritors.

One of the major challenges facing inheritors as they move into adulthood is that of raising their own children. It has been interesting and encouraging for me to see how often young people free themselves from the problems that tend to accompany inheritance when they become involved with the challenge and the excitement of raising their own children.

Wealthy young parents who feel wounded or diminished by their experience of inheritance can approach the nurturance of their children as a challenging opportunity to break the negative pattern of past generations.

Such parents often find great meaning in helping their own children to avoid some of the pitfalls and problems that they experienced. They can also find great satisfaction in seeing their children grow up less troubled by these problems and with sound values. They will also be aware that whatever they are able to accomplish with their children will probably be passed on to subsequent generations.

Peer groups are helpful to many.

Self-help groups that bring together people who share certain problems or situations are proving to be of great value to more and more people. In many communities there are groups for those who have inherited or expect to inherit wealth. These groups deal with a variety of problems and questions, including investment, charitable giving, and the kinds of issues discussed in this paper. Inheritors may find benefit in exploring existing groups of this kind and, if they don't find any that meet their needs, they may start their own. An experienced and trustworthy facilitator (who is not a participant) can be very helpful in creating a group that serves its members. Among other contributions, a skilled facilitator can help to provide an atmosphere that feels safe to the participants, can keep the discussion fruitfully centered, can ensure that all participants are heard, and can stimulate productive participation.

CONCLUSION

Inheriting substantial wealth is neither an unadulterated good nor a catastrophe. Problems do come with it, but an awareness of these problems, by caring and thoughtful parents and by the young people themselves, can go very far toward ameliorating them and making it possible for inheritors to live lives that are full, creative, and satisfying.

Confirmation of the idea that inheritance can be a blessing and not a curse can be seen in these quotes from two famous and wealthy fathers. President John Adams wrote to his wife, Abigail, in 1780: "My sons ought to study Mathematics, Commerce and Agriculture, in order to give their children a right to study painting, poetry and porcelain." Of course, one of these sons, John Quincy Adams, also became one of our Presidents. In his book, "The Jameses", R.W.B. Lewis writes about Henry Senior whose idea was to raise his children in what he called "an atmosphere of freedom," giving them every opportunity for expansion without expecting them to produce anything in particular. The achievements of his two sons, William and Henry James, made them major figures in psychology/philosophy and in fiction writing.

CHAPTER 2
Trusts Versus Trust

This Chapter focuses on the human side of trusts—those agreements that curiously enough, often connote lack of trust. It discusses some of the purposes for which trusts are written and how these can affect the lives of the people involved. It also offers some suggestions as to how the estate planning process can become more beneficial to all concerned.

This chapter is based on a talk given to the Estate Planning Division of the Bar Association of Santa Clara County (California). The purpose of my presentation was to help the attorneys better understand the effects, especially on young people, of inheriting substantial wealth, so that they could work with their parents to make the experience of inheritance as constructive as possible.

The issues involved in the transmission of major wealth are important, not only as they influence the people directly involved, but also because of their effects on the larger society. Financial professionals who work with the affluent are often in a position to make a real difference in the nature and consequences of the experience of inheriting. But many estate-planning professionals tend to concentrate too exclusively on the financial and legal issues—on matters such as avoiding taxes and safeguarding the fortune against dangers or foolishness. This can result in neglect of the human issues—the ways in which the inheritance of money affects people and their lives.

I know something about all this because I was an inheritor and because I've interviewed and worked with many other inheritors, affluent parents, and psychotherapists who have wealthy clients. Originating as a research project, my concern with the problems connected with inheritance has evolved into a career. Over the years, I've been consulting with inheritors, parents, financial professionals, and families about how best to make the inheritance experience a blessing and an opportunity, not a burden. My consulting work has focused on issues of living, as I do not offer legal or financial advice.

Why should a wealthy person go through the process of having a trust prepared? Why not just leave the money directly to one's beneficiaries? The following are six of the more common reasons for setting up trusts (and not necessarily what clients will say, or even be aware, are their reasons):

1. *Avoiding taxes*
2. *Concern with the children's welfare until they mature sufficiently*
3. *Preventing them from making costly mistakes*
4. *Guarding inheritors from the dangers in the world*
5. *Maintaining control over the children's lives*
6. *Establishing and continuing a dynasty*

The first reason for the use of trusts is **to avoid taxes**. Hardly anyone outside of the IRS is going to question this goal. Inheritors almost always approve of whatever can be done to minimize what goes to the tax collectors. There are exceptions. Not long ago I consulted with a family in which the father chose to pay an extra $100,000 in taxes in order to provide equity for his children. This man's father had set up trusts which had the effect of treating those children differently—which was unacceptable to my client—who considered the emotional impacts on his children as more important than the money itself.

A second reason for a trust is **to provide for the children until they are adequately mature**. This is a laudable motive but subject to misuse. For example, I know of a woman of 35 keeps asking her father when she's going to be mature enough to handle her own financial affairs. She feels strongly that his refusing to relinquish control of the money simply means that he doesn't trust or respect her, and this has caused her extreme suffering and led to years of psychoanalysis. (Psychotherapists are often the indirect beneficiaries of restrictive trust arrangements.) Her brothers are still struggling with their own maturation and alternating between subservience and rebelliousness toward their father. Seeing and treating young people as immature often serves as a self-fulfilling prophecy—they don't grow up. This kind of mistrust and over protectiveness applies particularly to daughters. A number of women clients have complained bitterly about how their fathers have withheld from them information and responsibilities which were given to their brothers.

A third reason for a trust is **to prevent one's children from making costly mistakes**. This is usually a well-intended objective but it can be damaging. Being overprotected and guarded generally delays children's maturation; they are so shielded from the world that they don't develop their psychological muscles. Risk taking is an essential ingredient of life, and particularly in growing up. We all learn from our mistakes, often painfully, but most of us don't seem able to do it in any other way. Excessive shielding is a major factor in the slow maturation of many inheritors. One symptom of this immaturity is indecisiveness and an inability to come to closure. This often is manifested in their dealings with their financial consultants, to an extent that many professionals find highly frustrating. Parents, and their estate planning consultants, need to balance the risk of wasting part of the inheritance against the children's development as responsible adults. To illustrate, a wealthy client employed a college friend to help him manage his investments. The friend succumbed to temptation and embezzled a considerable amount of the family money. But this experience, while extremely stressful and painful, was seen by all—including the inheritor's father—as an honest error on the heir's part, and one that was probably well worthwhile for what it taught all of them.

A fourth reason for setting up a trust is **to guard children from the dangers in the world**. This is a praiseworthy notion but the effects can be of dubious value. Certainly the world can be a dangerous place, and in some ways particularly so for the wealthy. Many people will take advantage of inheritors and use them, often in ways that are painful and disillusioning. An affluent man told me a proverb: "When a man of wealth and a man of experience get together, the man of experience gains wealth while the man of wealth gains experience."

Inheritors can and often do get involved with people and causes that are dubious—in terms of good judgment, ethics, and even legality. But this can be a valuable part of their learning and maturing process. When children are too protected against making their own errors this results in a number of unhappy and harmful effects—particularly a lack of self-confidence and self-esteem, and resentment toward their parents.

Wealthy parents usually provide their children with the best academic educations they can find, but too often they seem not to be aware of the importance of other kinds of education. Children need to learn about living—how to function in the world—and to learn about themselves. Such education comes mainly from life experience and often from making mistakes—and rarely from the advice of parents or teachers. Protecting children from such experiences can interfere with their education. Legal instruments that limit excessively the inheritors' choices can keep them from being adequately educated for living.

To illustrate, a young man with whom I worked married a prostitute. The marriage lasted only a few weeks and extricating him from the situation was expensive as well as painful. But as I came to know him it seemed clear that this was an important experience in learning and maturation for him, and he's now happily married and living a good life. Protecting him from this experience would certainly have saved money and suffering but, in my view, what he gained personally from this mistake was more than worth the cost.

A fifth reason to create a trust is **to maintain control over the children's lives.** Here the motives are often rather shadowy. Most of us want our children to be and to behave, as we would wish. Too often I find that this is translated into being as much like us as possible. But most parents know, or learn painfully, that this generally doesn't sit well with their children. Many inheritors have described with sadness and anger how their parents have held out the promise of inheritance—and the threat of disinheritance—so that they feel controlled and coerced. Trusts are often used in this way long after it is really appropriate, with money still being distributed on the basis of adult heirs behaving in ways that are deemed satisfactory to their parents or the trustees.

One way in which parents keep in control through trusts and other such documents is by setting up systems which are so intricate that it is nearly impossible for the inheritors to know where they stand even if they read the documents. A surprising number of wealthy young adults are in the dark about the extent of the family fortune, how much will come to them, in what form, and when. They know they are rich, but they don't know how rich. And they don't know when, if ever, they will have control over their own fortunes. This means, of course, that they will have difficulty planning their lives. Their perfectly natural response to being kept in this sort of ignorance is sadness and anger toward their parents, which hurts everyone.

One form of control that is potentially quite damaging is forcing children to work in the family business without taking into account their talents and inclinations. There are occasions when such work is right, when it's an opportunity for the inheritor. But many heirs spend their working lives in occupations that really do not suit them, at great cost to themselves, and often to others. For example, the dangers inherent in nepotism are well documented. Inheriting wealth should provide beneficiaries with freedom and opportunities, enabling them to choose their work and their lives. Too often parental coercion changes this potential blessing into a burden.

Of course, this whole issue is clouded with ambiguity. Children do need to demonstrate a certain level of maturity and competence before being given control over a great deal of money. But too often trusts operate in ways that go far beyond this. There is a clear and crucial difference between making the distribution of a fortune dependent on demonstrated maturity, and trying to fit children into a mold. The latter fails to honor the children or to permit them to develop and to live their own individuality—to be and to become who they really are. And it may drive them underground, pretending to be what they perceive as desired and hiding their true nature and many of their activities.

The sixth major reason for using trusts **is to establish and maintain a dynasty**. This is the motive with the greatest potential for damaging inheritors. Wealthy people can become quite captivated by the prospect of their name and their progeny going on through time as important and famous—the American equivalent of European aristocracy. While the stated, and perhaps even a real purpose for setting up the fortune in this way is usually to provide for the security and comfort of the grandchildren and great-grandchildren, too often it seems instead to be a form of self-aggrandizement. Perhaps a clue to this motive is that most such trust instruments are named after the donors, not the beneficiaries. Some wealthy people try for immortality by setting up monuments of various kinds, while others use trusts. But a much more satisfactory form of immortality is healthy, well-functioning children.

A very unfortunate result of a dynastic emphasis is that the young people feel, with some reason, that their parents' concern is for the fortune itself and may be greater than their caring for their children. This adds to their sense of not being trusted and not being loved—a painful and destructive combination.

A young couple, whose parents and grandparents had set up a dynastic system of trusts of extraordinary complexity and stringency, decided to leave their own money directly to their children, with no provision for their grandchildren. Their principal considerations in this decision were that it is important that their children know that it is up to them to provide for their own children, and that their parents trusted them to assume this responsibility, and in their own ways. In a family meeting I facilitated, two of the children wanted the money to come directly to them while the third felt that her children-to-be should have the satisfaction of knowing that their grandfather cared so much for her that he left her some of his money directly. They worked this out satisfactorily, but it kept them occupied for some time.

A wealthy father tried to force his four children to hold on to their fortunes, to operate as a family unit, and to make sure that they put more into the estate than they take out, for the sake of future generations. The children have found various ways of frustrating these demands, one of which is that three of the four have not, and probably will not have children of their own. They also are steadfastly refusing to have much to do with each other or to cooperate in maintaining and sharing the family properties.

Given all of these pitfalls and warnings, what is a responsible and caring estate planning professional to do about such thorny matters? Among a whole range of possibilities, here are some thoughts on ways in which you can help to make the process serve the people for whom it is intended, while strengthening, in the finest sense, your relationships with your clients. In considering these, it is essential to keep in mind that there are no simple answers and rarely is there only one right way. The estate planner must tune into and respond to individual situations. While formulas often work well with technical matters, they seldom apply so well to people, perhaps because we seem to insist on being individuals.

First, as you work with wealthy parents on wills, trusts, and the like, try always to **keep in mind the effects that these can have on the development and maturation of the beneficiaries**. As counselors, your responsibility includes a consideration of the human factors; much more is involved than drawing up documents which are "correct" and unassailable. Of course you need to do what you can to protect the estate and to see that the money is apportioned as desired. But you can do considerably more, including advising your clients as to the potential impact on their children of various ways of transferring and dealing with the wealth. Whether or not your clients follow your advice, you have a responsibility to offer it, and even to urge that they consider it seriously. Also, the occasions when clients are drawing up such documents are opportunities for them to clarify their values and to become more conscious of the effects on their loved ones, and you can help significantly in facilitating this process.

One way of exercising this advisory responsibility is to help clients to see that **creating wills and trusts is an opportunity for them, not just a duty**. Help them to realize that beyond the financial, legal and technical matters is a chance to make important personal statements. This is an ideal time for wealthy people to become clearer about their values and ideals—what really matters to them and what they want to give their lives to. Not only that, they can use the opportunity to communicate these values to those they care most about, something most of us don't ordinarily do very well. A well thought-out statement in a will or trust can have a great deal more impact than a mini-lecture delivered to one's children.

Second, keep conscious of the flaw, so common in trusts and wills, of **delaying too long in giving responsibility to the inheritors**. While you may never be criticized for taking the prudent way—doing all you can to safeguard the fortune and to protect against foolishness—this is not enough. You can also help parents to see that withholding responsibility and power from their heirs too long or too rigidly is likely to be bad for them. If their parents don't trust them, how can they trust or respect themselves? Obviously there are no simple answers here, but some parents have done well with various plans. One of these, among many, is dividing the inheritance into three segments (not necessarily equal), with the first going at age 21 and the other two following along at intervals of 5 to 10 years, often contingent on some demonstration of a developing ability to handle the money responsibly.

Third, encourage parents to **keep their children informed and to involve them in decisions regarding their inheritance**. Try to set up meetings with the children, the parents, you and perhaps other financial advisors, in which you can make presentations to them and can participate in discussions intended to clarify the factual situation and the points at issue. It is often useful for the family to hold one or more intergenerational meetings, without attorneys or other financial professionals, for open discussion of the estate planning process. In such meetings the children can be encouraged to ask questions, to express their concerns and feelings, and generally to converse freely with their parents and siblings, with an agreement that there are no taboo topics. Families often find that it is worth-while to bring in a skilled and objective outside facilitator (usually not the family attorney or other professional) to keep the conversation flowing, to ensure that topics of concern are covered, and that everyone has adequate opportunities to speak and to be heard. Involving the children doesn't mean democracy—the kids don't get an equal vote—but they should be heard and respected, and their views need to be considered as the parents make their decisions.

One of the most damaging and painful experiences for many large inheritors is the mystery and secrecy that has surrounded the wealth. This often gives the young people a sense that there is something wrong with it—that the money is bad or dirty—and also that they themselves cannot be trusted with information about it. When clients indicate that they believe that such knowledge should be withheld from their children, it is often useful to question them as to just what they fear might happen if their children were in possession of more information which will affect their lives. Further, it is important to do all that you can to be sure that female inheritors are treated the same as males in this process. Try to discourage your clients from behaving as though women can't be expected to understand finances. This is particularly the case in those not infrequent situations where a daughter is more competent in these matters than her brothers or even her father.

Fourth, **including a charitable element in trusts** can help the children to be aware of the importance of making philanthropy a significant part of their lives. I keep finding that those inheritors who lead productive and satisfying lives are surprisingly often the ones for whom philanthropy is a major value and activity. One wealthy young woman is going a long way toward solving her personal problems with her substantial inheritance by bringing to it a philanthropic focus in which she is giving to a cause that matters to her—not only a significant part of her money but also of her time and her talents. This has made her feel that her inheritance is justified, and that her life is meaningful and exciting.

Fifth, be more aware of, and more helpful with the **emotional stress** that most of your clients are experiencing while they are talking with you about wills and trusts. A great many people go through these events with considerable pain and fear, not only because this forces them to face their own mortality—that they really are going to die—but also because the decisions they are making have such important and emotion-laden consequences. Clients usually try to ignore or to hide such "unworthy" feelings and I've been told that most attorneys and other financial professionals tend to ignore and to avoid emotional issues.

In such situations it is important to do what you can to provide opportunities for feelings to come out into the open, and for them to be recognized as having a significant impact on the decisions made. An attorney friend who works in estate planning once said that he believes that he is doing his job properly when clients feel able to cry in his office appropriately. Avoiding or ignoring the powerful emotional forces which are at work in the estate planning process is not only depriving your clients of important opportunities in their own development, but it often results in their being unable to make rational decisions regarding their estates.

Finally, there is **no reason why wills and trusts can't be human**. You can play a very helpful role by letting your clients know that they can write personal statements of any length or nature and place them in these legal documents—statements about themselves and their values, and about their feelings and hopes for their beneficiaries. Parents often find much personal significance in the experience of putting such feelings and attitudes into words and communicating them to those they care most about. It is moving and impressive how important these messages can be to the beneficiaries, particularly since they are usually received at such critical and vulnerable times.

CHAPTER 3
An American Taboo
Or Why It Isn't All Right to Talk About Personal Wealth

If you're not sure that wealth is a taboo topic in our society, just ask someone close to you about his or her net worth or their annual income. Or, take a moment to imagine your reactions if someone were to ask you how much you own or what you earn.

Wealth in this culture seems to be an example of what sociologists call a *"taboo"*. We are intrigued by forbidden knowledge and yet we often contrast our practicality and rationality with the superstitious beliefs and ways of others. However, if we think we're free of such taboos, we need to take another look. For some mysterious reasons we've created a special taboo around money that is often powerful, irrational, and destructive. **Making** and **having** money are anything but taboo for us, especially in recent years. But **talking** about how much money we have is just not done. This secrecy can be particularly harmful in relationships—between parents and children. And our taboo against disclosing wealth does not apply only to the truly affluent; it also affects those of quite moderate means.

Taboo topics are intriguing. Sex is a fascinating subject for many, particularly when it's beyond the bounds of socially acceptable behavior. Many people are intrigued with articles and films about death and dying, another major taboo in our culture. And the popularity of articles and TV programs about the "Rich and Famous" as well as the annual listings of the wealthiest people in *Forbes* and *Fortune* magazines attest to the power and the fascination about personal wealth.

The taboo topic of wealth is of particular interest to me because I consult with individuals and families on issues related to inherited wealth. My function is to help them to make the prospect and the actuality of inheritance a positive experience for all—a blessing and not a curse. In this consulting I keep encountering situations where parents go to considerable expense, trouble and discomfort to conceal the magnitude of their fortunes. Sometimes this taboo-driven behavior simply creates a nuisance; yet, often serious harm is done, especially to inheritors. The damage includes bad financial decisions, inadequate preparation of young people to handle wealth responsibly, strained and distant relationships, poor self-esteem for inheritors, and the stress of maintaining and safeguarding secret knowledge.

Here are some examples, mostly from my own experience as a consultant, of the workings of this taboo and of the damage it often creates. (The names used in these examples are all fictitious.)

Henry, an apparently happily married man, has been forging his wife's signature to their joint tax returns for years to keep her from knowing his income. Aside from ethical considerations and the effect on their relationship, if he doesn't trust her it seems remarkably foolish and irrational of him to put her in a position where she could turn him in for income tax fraud.

Frank, participating in a group of wealthy parents, was urged to talk with his children about the family fortune and his plans for distributing his estate. After a few minutes of this he was clearly becoming so agitated that I was concerned for his health. Finally, red-faced and with great effort, he blurted out, "I won't tell them because it's none of their business." When others in the group tried to explain to him that, in fact, it was very much "their business," he angrily shut down and refused to listen any more.

The men (no women!) of the Jackson family meet annually to discuss various matters of shared concern. Toward the end of the meetings, before the review of financial statements and consideration of family investments, the younger men are politely told to leave the room, as the elders will deal with these matters. It doesn't seem odd to the seniors that the "young men" have grown into their 50's and even 60's.

Bill, a financial planner, told me of being employed by the Mitchells, an elderly couple who told him their holdings totaled some two million dollars. After they'd met together a few times, they conceded that the figure was closer to five million dollars. Still later, when Tim, the husband, left the room for a moment, his wife, Helen, leaned over and whispered to the financial man "Actually it's eleven million." Bill was bemused by the mistrust this secrecy demonstrated, but even more by the cost to the couple of his needing to change investment strategies according to his understanding of the amount of their available funds. He told me he was still wondering just what the true magnitude of their fortune might be.

When Marjorie consulted me, she said she was so controlled by her fear of appearing wealthy that she lived far beneath her means and her wishes. Even so, there were certain friends and working associates who were never invited to her home because it might seem too affluent to them. The costs to her in time, effort, and the continuing discomfort of living a lie were great. As we explored the likely consequences of her letting people know that she was wealthy, she eased considerably in her concealment and became more comfortable with revealing that she is a woman of wealth. And, somewhat to her surprise, she's been finding that her wealth doesn't seem to be a significant issue to most people; they're not that interested.

Many wealthy parents go to great lengths (and expense) to conceal their wealth from their children. This often takes the form of complex and restrictive trust documents that are often unavailable to the heirs. The children usually know that such trusts exist and are intended for their eventual benefit. But they are ignorant as to the amounts and the terms (e.g., when, if ever, they will have access to the principal funds). This usually engenders pain at not being trusted and respected—and anger toward their parents.

And, of course, it makes it more difficult for the young people to plan their lives.

Peter told me that he didn't want his children to know just how wealthy the family was, because this would diminish their initiative and because the wealth might be gone by the time they were ready to inherit. Since the parents took pride in their four showplace homes, the fact of their wealth might not have come as a complete surprise to his children.

Family offices are organizations set up to perform various financial and other services for members of wealthy families. In a number of these, senior family members have instructed the office staff not to divulge information about family or personal wealth to members of the younger generations. Such a situation hurts the younger people's ability to make life decisions, and it lowers their self-esteem.

Many parents have developed effective ways of discouraging their children from asking questions about the size of the family fortune—particularly about what might be coming to them, when and how. While parents' motives for such avoidance may be benign, such censorship often operates in damaging ways. The children feel guilty and sinful (selfish) for asking such questions, and they sense that there is something wrong with the topic, and with them for being interested in it. Unfortunately, such attitudes are often transmitted through the generations.

In exploring the nature of this taboo I have discovered several reasons the wealthy give for hiding the extent of their affluence—particularly from the young people who will be affected. Most of these reasons apply, perhaps with less intensity, to those of only moderate wealth. All the reasons have some validity; they're not simply rationalizations. However, none of them, separately or together, come close to explaining the intensity of the prohibition experienced against revealing information about wealth. They don't account for the severity, the passion, and the disregard for the consequences evoked in so many people simply by the prospect of violating this taboo.

Some reasons I've been given for maintaining the silence surrounding personal wealth, especially with one's children, are:

"Talking about wealth is in poor taste. Nice people just don't do it."

For the most part this is true; "nice" people usually don't talk about their money, but what does that mean? Who made the decision that it's in "poor taste" to talk about one's wealth? Obviously, boasting is distasteful. But the offense is in the flaunting, **not** the money. And the dubious commitment to "good taste" hardly justifies keeping one's children ignorant, confused and troubled.

"If our children know how wealthy we are, and what they are likely to inherit, it will damage them."

The danger most often cited here is low motivation, especially for work. What this can really mean is that the parents want their children to make a lot of money, for dynastic purposes or out of a conviction that this is the best thing to do with one's life. Making money may be the best career for some young people, but it certainly isn't for all. Also, I keep observing that, regardless of wealth, children who are raised with a healthy work ethic do not grow up to be indolent or frivolous; they accept demanding challenges with enthusiasm.

Another reason I've heard is that their offspring aren't mature enough to deal with being wealthy, which means that they will spend the money foolishly, live self-indulgently or be taken advantage of by promoters and friends. Such parental attitudes serve as self-fulfilling prophecies: treating young people as immature tends to keep them that way. Overly cautious parents ignore the reality that people learn by making mistakes, so depriving children of such opportunities is interfering with their life education, and in a very damaging way.

"If my children know, they'll just be waiting for me to die so they can get their hands on my money."

Sadly, this can be a self-fulfilling prophecy. Treating children with mistrust isn't likely to make them very loving toward their parents. Also, this "cautious" attitude reflects another major taboo in our culture: dealing with our own mortality—that we really are going to die some day. Those who can't face this reality for themselves are likely to go to some lengths to avoid discussing it. But the fears of discussing these taboo topics—wealth and death—almost always turn out to be far less justified than expected. When parents do talk with their children about inheritance matters and the feelings involved, it's usually beneficial for all concerned. And in my experience, the discomfort experienced is short-term and not as intense as was feared.

"If people know how much I've got, this will give them power over me."

The nature of this power is usually unclear, but many wealthy people experience a vague fear that "they" will somehow take it away. Therefore, disclosing their wealth makes them feel exposed and vulnerable to being hurt in some way. Furthermore, it's often not at all clear who the threatening "they" are, which can be even more frightening.

"I'm embarrassed (or ashamed) to have people know how wealthy I am."

This attitude is more common among those with inherited fortunes than those who made theirs and it has both an inner and an outer aspect. Inwardly, people may feel they're not entitled to be so much better off than others ("Why me?"). Hiding their wealth is a way, though not a very effective one, of avoiding this painful confrontation with their own sense of guilt. Outwardly, a person may fear that his or her wealth would induce in others reactions of envy, judgment, obsequiousness and anger—damaging their relationships, to say the least. Also this touches on one of the basic fears of wealthy people—that they can't trust the motives of people with whom they relate. While some justification for this fear does exist, it's generally significantly exaggerated. People who come out of the closet about their wealth usually find that most others aren't very surprised or even very interested. And those who respond badly are likely to turn out to be people they don't really want in their lives anyway.

"If people know of my wealth, it will create a barrier between us."

The fear is that people will view a wealthy person as somehow different, alien, and distant from them. Such reactions interfere with friendships as well as with working relationships. Of course this can happen, but it's not true of most people, and when it does, the barriers are probably not insuperable.

"If people know how much I have or what I earn, I'll be involved in a competition and judged by how I score in this game."

This rationale reflects a peculiarity in our society—our competitiveness around money matters. Many people do judge others by their wealth. Interestingly, "What is he/she worth?" is understood to refer solely to fiscal assets—not to the other qualities that determine personal "worth." Revealing one's wealth will elicit competitive and judging reactions from some people. So, each must decide how important this factor is—how painful and destructive it might be to be evaluated by this irrational criterion—and how significant are the people who do judge this way.

Since these reasons, and others, fall far short of explaining the intensity of the wealth taboo, we have something mysterious operating here—a hallmark of a true taboo. The irrational prohibitions surrounding wealth are omnipresent in our society. The lengths to which people go to maintain secrecy and the costs they pay in money, time, effort, and human consequences to themselves and their children are astonishing. We could speculate about hidden reasons, but it seems more useful to consider what might be done to reduce the power of the taboo against talking about one's wealth.

In considering this, I am not suggesting that everyone should go about telling anyone who will listen about their income and net worth. The key issue here is appropriateness. There's no point in revealing or discussing one's personal wealth in situations where there isn't a sound reason for doing so. But it can be valuable to be able to talk about personal wealth where it does make sense, without being inhibited by irrational, even superstitious fears.

The most important situations where it is useful to discuss wealth openly are between parents and their heirs. The examples I've observed where harm is done by this taboo mostly involve people of substantial wealth, but it can be just as important for parents of moderate means to be open on this topic with their children.

It would be nice to believe that, once people understood that something as irrational and harmful as this taboo is operating in their lives, they would see the foolishness of it and change their attitudes and ways. But the nature of a taboo is that it resists reason and logical arguments. An effective way to avoid such confrontations is to deny that a taboo exists at all and to insist that "rational" reasons adequately explain such secretive behavior. Despite the intensity of this taboo, I believe that it is possible to reduce the pervasiveness and the power of this prohibition. I wouldn't try to argue anyone out of their beliefs on this subject (or perhaps anything else). But I am convinced that opening up the subject and encouraging people to examine their beliefs and their reasons for maintaining this secrecy, as well as looking at the damage for which it is responsible, can minimize the taboo, at least to an extent.

As psychotherapists know, increasing consciousness about how we operate produces change—particularly in our counter-productive attitudes and strategies. As people are able to see what the wealth taboo costs them, and as they realize that the disastrous consequences they foresee in going public are greatly exaggerated, they will be able to regain the control over their lives.

One suggestion, easier to propose than to follow, is that people of means take the risk of beginning to violate the taboo. This can be a gradual process, beginning with small risks—divulging a little information and to people who seem particularly trustworthy. The point is to observe the effects—to learn first-hand whether the feared consequences of these violations happen. My prediction (based on my own experience as well as that of others with whom I've worked) is that the consequences, with rare exceptions, will not prove harmful, perhaps not even painful. In fact, I predict that the opposite will generally be true, that beneficial results can be expected, such as improved relationships, growing trust, and enhanced self-esteem. And the initial and anticipated stress will give way to comfort, perhaps even euphoria.

In my consulting practice, I usually encourage parents, and children, to talk together about these issues, often beginning by considering the barriers against this, including their feelings of discomfort and apprehension. We discuss the nature of the taboo, consider its irrational elements, and look at the actual and potential damage to which it can lead. Then the parents may be ready to move to a sharing of hard information—facts about the size and the nature of the family assets.

This is often followed by a discussion of the parents' estate planning. I use the word "discussion" advisedly here, since I believe that parents should consider their children's wishes and ideas in planning the distribution of their estates. Families often find that bringing in a professional facilitator to provide a skilled and objective presence can greatly ease the tension and improve the quality of communication. My experience has been that where estate planning is seen as a joint family enterprise, including all of the people centrally involved in the decisions, the results are always superior, both in terms of the quality of the plan developed and of the relationships within the family.

In suggesting that parents move against the wealth taboo, I acknowledge, of course, that there are cases and times where it truly is prudent for parents to be somewhat secretive about their wealth and their estate planning. Usually this involves making a judgment about one or more of their children—that they are currently incapable of handling this sort of information without damage to themselves or others. With these very rare exceptions, in all of my experience of dealing with the wealthy, I have yet to see a case where harm was done by providing too much information, too early, to children. And I have observed very many situations where withholding was destructive, even tragically so.

I also wish to make clear that in calling attention to this secretive behavior on the part of so many wealthy parents I am not indicting or criticizing them. This taboo is a pervasive phenomenon in our culture, and it is inevitable that people will be influenced by it. The point is not to assign blame, not even so much to understand its roots, (though this can be interesting), but to do what we can to reduce the power of this prohibition and the harm which it does. I'm convinced that we can do a great deal in this respect, and that many people will be much better off as a result.

CHAPTER 4
Wealth and Wisdom

The following reflections on wisdom and wealth have emerged from a personal quest to cultivate my own wisdom. Over the years, my personal quest has become an important aspect of the consulting work that I do with affluent individuals and families. I've become increasingly aware that wisdom is particularly important in the lives of wealthy people, guiding them in their decisions about how they spend their money, how they disseminate their money philanthropically, and how they ultimately transmit their wealth to their heirs.

This chapter begins by exploring—and differentiating among—three capacities: *intellectual power, knowledge,* and *wisdom.* I then move on to consider *wisdom* itself and the characteristics that are evident in people we generally consider wise. Finally, I discuss how wisdom is specifically relevant to affluent people in their overall utilization of wealth.

WHAT IS INTELLIGENCE?

We all talk about *intelligence*, and most of us would like a bit more of it, but what do we really mean by it? What we ordinarily characterize as one trait—that of "intelligence"—seems to be comprised of three quite different qualities. Though often lumped together, these three aspects of intelligence are equally involved in the accumulation and use of wealth, as will be discussed later in this chapter.

The first of the qualities we attribute to be intelligence is ***intellectual power*** or ***mental acuity***. This capacity is what intelligence tests attempt to measure, and it's what we usually think we mean when we describe "intelligence." But current thought has revealed that there are many types of mental ability, with the "IQ" or Intelligence Quotient test only defining the most academic. "Street smarts" or emotional intelligence involving the ability to understand and relate to people, the mental agility of a fine athlete, an esthetic sensibility—though difficult to measure and often ignored or devalued—are all aspects of a larger view of intelligence and mental processing ability.

Intellectual power seems largely to be genetically determined, though research shows that we rarely use more than a fraction of our inherent capacities. But, whatever our natural endowments, our native powers can be developed through discipline and training. Just as athletes work with their inherent gifts to maximize them, so too can we develop and improve our mental powers through effort, study and guidance.

The second quality included under "intelligence" is **knowledge**. This includes access to factual information but it goes far beyond. We acquire knowledge as we master an occupation, as we understand more about the nature of our world, and as we learn about ourselves and other human beings. And though we use our cognitive abilities to learn, but intellectual capacity is not at all the same as knowledge. For example, we've all known people of clearly superior mental gifts who don't seem to know very much.

WHAT IS WISDOM?

The first two aspects of intelligence—intellectual power and knowledge—are reasonably easy to describe, but wisdom is rather ineffable. One of the most useful, respected and classic works on wisdom is the *Tao Te Ching*, written by Lao Tse in China some 2,500 years ago. These writings encourage us to live according to the *Tao*, and much of the book is devoted to describing and illustrating the various meanings of *Tao*. Lao Tse also says this about the *Tao*: *"Those who know don't say; those who say don't know."* This is one of the many paradoxes in this little book, and it seems that wisdom teachings often require paradoxical expressions.

Wisdom doesn't necessarily accompany the other aspects of what we call intelligence. Many people we don't see as being very gifted intellectually demonstrate wisdom in their lives. T.S. Eliot recognized this difference in his lines: *"Where is the wisdom we have lost in knowledge? Where is the knowledge we have lost in information?"* A friend who worked for years in a highly respected think tank was led to the conclusion that "Intelligence is no cure for stupidity."

Knowledge and intellectual power are qualities we have, but wisdom is something we are, and can be transformed by. Knowledge can be taught, while wisdom is often gained through direct experience or modeled by the wise, so that we can learn it.

While wisdom can't truly be defined, it is still possible to make a few remarks about it. I offer these in the fairly certain knowledge that as I mature in my own wisdom, these descriptions will change for me. And I do recognize the validity of Lao Tse's observation that "Those who say don't know"—so that by setting down the following views I may be admitting that I don't know very much about wisdom.

Wisdom is what it takes to make good choices in life—to recognize options, to distinguish among them, and to select and follow those that will be most creative and rewarding. Jonas Salk, who discovered the cure for polio, said "I have defined wisdom as the capacity to make judgments that when looked back upon will seem to have been wise."

Choosing wisely often requires us to break out of the habitual "either/ or" approach to decision-making, to seek and to recognize other alternatives. Wisdom sees **wholes**—the forest and not just the trees—while recognizing the importance of the parts—the trees and not just the forest. Thus the wise are able to put situations and problems into realistic perspective.

Being wise means being conscious of our own **limitations**—that our days are only 24 hours and that we won't live forever, at least in this body. Accepting this reality means that every choice we make means saying No to other options. As we get wiser we become more conscious in setting priorities for our choices and our lives, relinquishing those paths and activities that are not ultimately rewarding. Such relinquishments are often particularly difficult for wealthy persons who may have become accustomed to having whatever they want.

Wisdom takes the **long view**: the wise person has the patience and vision to defer short-term gratifications and to accept some discomfort in order to follow paths and goals of lasting value.

Humility accompanies wisdom. Competitiveness and self-aggrandizement block us from living at our highest level. As we grow wiser, we are more willing and able to accept and to show ourselves as we are, free of needs to make ourselves seem better—to others or to ourselves. Becoming increasingly non-attached to how we are judged is wonderfully freeing in enabling us to pursue goals that are much more satisfying. Humility enables persons to become good listeners, which probably helps them to become wiser.

A characteristic of many people who seem truly wise is a central concern with the **spiritual dimension** of life—a concern that underlies their values. This may, but doesn't necessarily imply practicing a *religion*, in the sense of a body of seekers united in a common structure and system. Spiritual, to me, describes the individual search for meaning and transcendence, and it involves an interest in and conviction of a reality beyond the material and mundane. Wise people experience themselves as being on a spiritual journey, centrally concerned with deepening their understanding of life's meaning and purpose, and living accordingly.

Humor is an attribute that characterizes the wise people I have known, and known of. Wisdom brings an ability to avoid earnestness, to treat our misfortunes and failings with some amusement, to get beyond self-importance, and to refuse to take ourselves too seriously. Wise persons may be intensely committed to their inner and their outer work, but this is accompanied by an ability to view it all from a somewhat detached, humorous perspective. This understanding is basic to many spiritual teachings.

Wisdom recognizes and values **relatedness**. As we grow wiser we become increasingly conscious of our interconnectedness—with those close to us, with the people of the planet, and with all life. Wisdom means growing beyond our skin-bound ego, and the sense of separateness with which most of us live, at least the first part of our life. Wisdom involves an awareness and appreciation of the power of love, as that which gives life its meaning and vitality. Love and relatedness are basic to the teachings of world religions and the finest spiritual teachers.

Wisdom recognizes and values our **intuitive capacities**. We don't have to deny or diminish the importance of our conceptual powers, but as we grow in wisdom we also grow in our ability to trust what our intuition tells us.

Wise people value and work at **self-understanding** and self-acceptance, recognizing the importance of growing in conscious appreciation of who we are. We can become increasingly aware of our motivations, our fears and concerns, as well as our prejudices—all contribute toward knowing who we truly are. In furthering self-understanding, there is wisdom in seeking good counseling and guidance, from psychotherapists, spiritual teachers and others—and not just for dealing with personal problems but also for enhancing the quality of life.

Growing in wisdom means becoming increasingly willing and able to **accept responsibility** for our own lives. Blaming others for our misfortunes and failures becomes increasingly irrelevant and uninteresting.

Most of us, in roughly the first half of life, work at growing in competence by developing our intellectual capacities and knowledge. As we become older, many of us find that these goals recede in importance and in the satisfaction they provide, and we are less motivated to pursue them. Life teaches us, in all sorts of ways, that becoming wiser is our most valued and desired purpose, and the one most worthy of our efforts. This shift toward wisdom can come about as we become bored and dissatisfied with other goals, or it can happen because we find a wise mentor—living or dead.

WISDOM AND WEALTH

The way we deal with our wealth represents a particularly significant aspect of life where the qualities that make up "intelligence" come into play. Making and preserving a fortune requires intellectual capacity and knowledge. To be financially successful, we must be astute at evaluating situations, anticipating developments and trends, making sound judgments about people and organizations, and understanding financial documents and other data. While some wisdom may be entailed here, these abilities call primarily on intellectual capacity and knowledge.

Using our wealth well, however, requires wisdom. Decisions about where and how to spend our money call for good judgment, a sense of our own priorities and values and, often, a willingness to forego immediate gratifications.

Wisdom is especially necessary in the process of estate planning. Determining how much to leave to one's heirs, in what time frame and with what restrictions, calls on all the wisdom we can muster. The sage person gives careful consideration to the **process** of estate planning—the ways in which these important decisions are made and who is involved in them. People who are good at making and preserving money often use their intellectual capacities and knowledge in developing an estate plan that minimizes taxes, but that may not serve the heirs as well as a wiser plan—one that takes into account the donor's personal values and priorities and the effects on the recipients.

Wise parents see that their children are trained in the management and use of wealth. They allow them to make mistakes, knowing that this is one of the principal ways in which wisdom is developed.

Giving money away—deciding how, and how much, to contribute philanthropically and where it should go—are choices much more dependent on wisdom than on intellectual power or knowledge (although these are also involved). Perhaps this is why Andrew Carnegie, late in life, realized that it was a great deal more difficult to give money away well than to make it. I keep discovering that affluent people, who demonstrate wisdom in their lives, take their philanthropic responsibilities and involvement very seriously. They study potential beneficiary organizations just as though they were considering investing to make money—in fact they tend to see philanthropy as investing, not for their own profit but toward supporting their values. They use their wisdom with the awareness of their own priorities, their vision of what can make a difference in the world, and their judgment of the organizations and individuals who are potential beneficiaries, so that their giving can be most effective and lastingly satisfying.

One of the best summary statements of the ineffable quality we call wisdom comes again from the *Tao Te Ching:* "It is more important to see the simplicity, to realize one's true nature, to cast off selfishness and temper desire." Can we help each other toward this goal?

CHAPTER 5
Is it Better to Give than to Receive?

In all my years of working as a consultant with wealthy individuals and families, I have become increasingly convinced that, other than choosing good parents, the best thing that can happen to someone who inherits substantial wealth is to be philanthropically involved. As an inheritor myself, I've also found that my participation in philanthropy—contributing money, time and talents, has been one of the very most rewarding and satisfying elements in my life.

Although the following discussion applies primarily to those who inherited their fortunes, it is also relevant for those who have earned their wealth through their own talents and find their lives significantly enriched by their philanthropic activities. Giving is especially rewarding for successful people who have retired. Their lives have been largely focused on work and on raising a family; withdrawal often brings boredom, depression and a sense of meaninglessness—problems similar to those which can afflict those who inherit their wealth.

There are a number of difficulties that can plague those who grow up and live with affluence—low self-esteem, guilt, delayed maturation, a sense of meaninglessness, boredom, lack of strong and sustained motivation, suspiciousness and alienation. These, however, are not inevitable burdens for beneficiaries, and philanthropic involvement usually provides a major contribution toward getting past such problems. In my work with wealthy individuals and families, I am repeatedly impressed at how often those inheritors who lead productive and satisfying lives are the ones for whom philanthropy is a major value and a significant element in their living.

Involvement in philanthropy can take many rewarding forms, much more than just writing checks in response to appeals or engaging in some form of planned giving. Wealthy people, particularly inheritors and those who have retired from making money, have the opportunity of making philanthropy a major focus of their lives, and of doing it proactively, not just responding to solicitations. I have known a number of inheritors who have made this a true and satisfying career, becoming professionally qualified as donors of their own wealth and sometimes that of their families and others.

Some guilt, which may or may not be conscious, seems rather inevitable as those who inherit large sums confront their own good fortune in a world of scarcity, suffering and deprivation. There are many ineffectual ways of dealing with this guilt; primarily attempts to prevent it from becoming very conscious. My own experience and observations show that becoming truly free of such existential guilt seems to require that inheritors develop a sense of stewardship around their use of their wealth, enabling them to feel that they are using their good fortune responsibly and generously.

Thoughtful and effective philanthropy can provide an exciting challenge to wealthy persons who might otherwise find themselves mired in aimlessness and boredom. Sharing their wealth with those who can make good use of it—not just the needy but also those individuals and institutions working toward the betterment of society—helps the affluent to feel that they are using their privilege constructively and not just selfishly. This not only reduces any guilt for their good fortune (the "Why me?" issue), but it also brings a sense of meaning and purpose to their lives and to their affluence.

Thoughtful philanthropists realize that, in many ways, the improvement of our society is dependent on philanthropy. Governments are very limited in what they can support and they tend to have a vested interest in the status quo. If our world is to become more just, sustainable and compassionate, it will require significant changes in our attitudes and practices, and philanthropy can provide support to the individuals and organizations that are working toward such changes.

Andrew Carnegie found, late in his life, that giving away money intelligently was more difficult than making it. There are a number of criteria to help donors determine if they are giving wisely. One of these, which I've found very useful, is gratitude. I've learned in my own contributing, and I often suggest to clients, that when we give judiciously, we neither expect nor want to be thanked. Instead we want to express our thanks.

Wise and appropriate philanthropy reflects and is an expression of our values. When we contribute to an organization, we are employing people to do what we believe should be done, what we want done. Often these people are performing these services (for us who employ them) at a significantly lower income than they could command elsewhere. If our giving is wise, we will want to thank them, not vice versa. And if we find that we desire expressions of appreciation, this probably indicates that our giving does not reflect our deepest and strongest values and is not supporting organizations or people to carry these values out. It can also mean that our motives are inappropriate, such as seeking personal prestige.

Actor Alan Alda has written, in a speech given to the Council on Foundations and printed in the newsletter of The Philanthropic Initiative: "I think something happens to us when we give. There's a better self in us that comes to the surface, gasping for air; glad to be let out." Later he writes: "So, I've come to believe that giving feels good, but I think giving strategically feels terrific." He goes on to point out that responsible philanthropy depends on answering a few key questions: "Why do we give?," "How much should we give?", "Where should we give?", and "How should we give?."

Responsible giving requires first that donors become clear about their personal values and priorities. This is something that most of us rarely do very consciously; we fail to recognize that what we value determines so much of what we do and how we live. Requiring ourselves to be more aware of what we care about not only makes us better philanthropists but also more conscious, more effective and happier people.

If donors are to choose the forms of philanthropy that are most relevant to each of them—to become wise in their giving—it is helpful to consider the various purposes served by individuals and organizations that are potential beneficiaries. Each person who volunteers money and time will find him or herself more drawn to some of these than to others. Donors are challenged to discover and then to focus their money, creativity, and efforts on those that arouse their passion and enthusiasm.

Here is one way of categorizing philanthropic purposes, with illustrative examples (listed in no particular order):

- Direct relief of suffering. (e.g. feeding and housing the indigent homeless.)
- Correcting the causes of suffering (e.g. helping the indigent to become employable, by augmenting their skills and their ability to find work).
- Dealing with social problems that cause suffering (e.g. failure of our educational system to prepare people to be employable).
- Alleviating injustice against individuals and groups (e.g. discrimination against various minorities).
- Improving educational opportunities for certain social groups and/or for everyone (e.g. better schools and teachers, at all levels).
- Advancement of human knowledge (e.g. scientific research and teaching).
- Working to avert and ameliorate catastrophes (e.g. wars, ecological disasters).
- Improving the quality of life through cultural enhancement (e.g. the arts).

• Helping to create a sustainable future (e.g. education and action to prevent environmental degradation and to support conservation and resource preservation).

• Working toward improved health and longevity (e.g. medical research).

• Fostering the spiritual development of individuals and groups (e.g. supporting spiritually oriented institutions and activities).

Within these categories of philanthropic purpose, giving one's money, time and talents can take the form of direct gifts to individuals who are in need, contributions to institutions which are providing services directly to people, or support of organizations that are working to bring about constructive changes in the society and its activities.

As donors become more clear about their values and priorities, it is important for them to choose and monitor those organizations and individuals that can best carry out the ideals to which they are committed. This can be an exciting challenge to the wealthy person who lacks motivation and who finds life somewhat empty and lacking in significance. Giving away money should be just as thoughtful an act as investing it. In fact, philanthropy can be considered a form of investing; it doesn't produce a financial return but it does bring other returns that can be at least as rewarding.

The greatest benefits usually come to donors who involve themselves actively and enthusiastically in the causes in which they believe. Serving on non-profit boards and helping with fund-raising are traditional and often rewarding activities for the wealthy. Some find additional meaning and gratification in more hands-on participation, such as using their skills, their enthusiasm and their contacts as volunteer consultants to the organizations they wish to support. For some, working as unpaid staff for one or more of the organizations they've chosen brings a very satisfying sense of meaning in life and of accepting the responsibilities that accompany wealth, whether earned or inherited.

A middle-aged, unmarried woman came to me for consultation because her life felt empty and meaningless. As we talked it became clear that she was deeply committed to her alma mater, which she supported with significant gifts. As we explored further, it developed that she had a passionate interest in a particular field of education that she believed was not being adequately researched and taught. After a good deal of consideration and discussion, she decided not only to endow a chair in that field but also to offer her services as a volunteer, helping to put together and to maintain that program. The changes in her vitality and her enthusiasm for living have been remarkable.

Deciding how much to give is, for many, a difficult, even painful process. I'm aware that these are intensely personal decisions, but I keep finding, with myself and others, that going a bit beyond what feels safe and comfortable brings surprising rewards. For affluent donors, I highly recommend a book, *Wealthy and Wise* (Little, Brown, 1994), by San Francisco investment manager Claude Rosenberg. In addition to making a powerful case for the importance of private philanthropy, he uses his financial expertise and considerable research, on data from the Internal Revenue Service and other sources, to show that most wealthy people can afford to give away considerably more than they do, without endangering their own or their children's security or comfort.

For some, a family foundation can be a wonderful vehicle for working collaboratively and enhancing communication and relationships, between and within generations. As described by Alan Alda, foundation meetings help family members to discover and define more clearly for themselves their deepest and most personal values. Expressing these in the family helps them all to understand each other better, to reduce divisive tensions, and to become closer. This process is described eloquently in a pamphlet about the foundation of the Graham family of Carmel, California: Building Family Unity Through Giving: The Story of the Namaste Foundation, (written by

Dianne Stone and published by the Whitman Institute, P.O. Box 2528, San Francisco, CA 94126; 415-982-0386).

Family foundations can also provide their members, particularly the young, with very valuable opportunities to learn and to grow—especially as they find what they most want to support, research the field, and then must make persuasive presentations to the family.

For those whose level of giving does not justify setting up a family foundation with all the expense and administrative responsibilities that this entails, Donor Advised Funds can be a fine substitute. These can be set up in Community Foundations (which exist in most areas), where a sum of money is given over to the community foundation, and the donors periodically inform the foundation of how much of this fund they wish to have contributed to the non-profit organizations they wish to support.

In summary, philanthropic involvement, particularly when it goes beyond monetary giving, is very significantly beneficial to the wealthy. In addition to the estate planning and tax advantages available, donors who give wisely, reflecting their personal values and thoughtful planning, find the quality of their lives enhanced. Inheritors in particular find such involvement to be a major factor in ameliorating the potentially damaging consequences of anticipating and of coming into fortunes. But thoughtful and active philanthropy is also highly gratifying and rewarding to the retired and to those still actively earning wealth—to all of us who are privileged to be able to give.

CHAPTER 6
How Much is Enough?

One of life's most important choices is one we usually don't make deliberately. Or, more accurately, we do make this choice in the ways we live our lives, but rarely is this done very consciously. Those of us privileged to live beyond the level of economic survival have the choice of deciding just how far above this level we want to go, and how important are the benefits of greater relative affluence. We all want "enough" money, but we're rarely clear as to what we mean by this.

The quality of our life depends largely on the ways we choose to spend our time and energy, both of which are more limited than we may like to realize. How much of these precious resources go into amassing money powerfully impacts the kind of life we live. We often base our answers to key questions that shape our life largely on what we consider to be "enough" money. These questions may include:

- What career will I choose?
- How hard will I work?
- Where will I live?
- What sort of life partner will I choose?
- How many children will I have?
- How much do I want to leave for my children?
- How will I spend the time that is available for my choices?
- How will I select my friends and companions?
- How much of my income will I put aside for the future?
- How speculative will I be in my investing?

• How important is philanthropy in my values?

When we think about it, we realize that the ways we answer such questions are based largely on what we consider to be "enough money." We seldom recognize that the question of enough is a major basis for our decisions, because we haven't faced this question very consciously. It's rare for any of us to look directly at the issue of how much wealth is enough for us. When we do, we often find that we are living our lives based on an answer that may have been valid much earlier in our lives, but which, with another look, seems no longer to fit us.

I've been fortunate in my lifetime to have had opportunities to associate with people with widely varying personal answers to the "How much is enough?" question. I've known and worked with individuals who have consciously chosen to live as close to the subsistence level as they could manage. For some this was an ethical choice—they were not comfortable having more than the necessities because of their awareness of those in need, or because they didn't wish to contribute more than necessary to our ecological problems. For others, living as simply as possible enabled them to have time and energy for pursuits which mattered more to them than material wealth—such as artistic pursuits, relationships with family and others, hobbies, volunteering for causes and people they wished to support.

At the other end of the spectrum, as a consultant to wealthy individuals and families, I've known people for whom the word "enough" didn't seem to have any meaning. We've all read about some of the more spectacular of these individuals who unaccountably risk disgrace and prison in the pursuit of additional wealth for which they seemingly have no use. Others, while not breaking any laws, seem so obsessed with accumulating wealth that they have neither the time nor the inclination to enjoy its rewards.

We can look at this life choice as selecting a place on a spectrum of wealth—from the minimum required to sustain life to a maximum that approaches the infinite. We choose, consciously or not, where on this spectrum we wish to live our lives. And whatever choice we make brings certain rewards as well as the payment of certain prices.

Those whose answer to "How much is enough?" is near the low end may gain free time to devote to their deepest concerns and values, and, possibly, an easy conscience. For this they are willing to accept the price of giving up some security, certain comforts, and status within the mainstream culture. Those whose goal is nearer the top end of the spectrum gain security for themselves and their families, status and prestige, and a comfortable, even luxurious life style. But these rewards usually come at the expense of free time and other benefits that could enhance their lives.

I don't believe that there is an objectively "right" answer to the question—only a personal one. Each of us aims for a position on this spectrum of wealth for our own reasons, based on who we are and on our personal values. The important issue is not a general, "How much is enough?" but, "How do I decide what is right for me, at this point in my life?" In answering this question for ourselves, it's valuable to look at various reasons for having more than we absolutely need, such as:

• **Security:** Protection for one's self and family against potential disasters, such as illness and injury, unemployment, economic decline.

• **Comfort and pleasure:** Enhancing our lives with possessions and experiences beyond the necessities.

• **Prestige:** The rewards that come with being admired and respected.

• **Competitiveness:** A way to keep score, assuming "Making money is the best game in town."

• **Philanthropy:** The satisfaction of being able to support activities and people that we care about and who represent our deepest values.

• **Power:** The ability to get things done—for ourselves, our family and friends, and our world.

• **Future Generations:** The privilege of being able to provide the benefits of affluence to our children and theirs.

If each of us needs to answer the "How much is enough?" question, and if there aren't any "right" answers that fit us all, then how do we go about finding our own resolution? The point here is to make our choice as conscious as we are able, so that the way we live our lives truly reflects our personal values and provides us the most satisfaction. Clearly this entails some inward searching—never an easy task. Facing this question seems particularly difficult for many of us.

The first step is to find out, as best we can, the nature of the decision we've been living with, however unconsciously. Looking at our life choices, what seems to have been our underlying assumption as to how much is enough?

If we are to find our own answer to the question, then we are challenged to do what we can to free ourselves from what others have tried to convince us. We may have been exposed to ideas and people counseling voluntary simplicity—living in ways that are outwardly simple and inwardly rich. We've also been exposed, from the media and elsewhere, to the notion that more is always better. If we are to find our own way, we need to look at these teachings, consider them on their merits, and then work at becoming free of their undue and unconscious influence.

Even more difficult, and perhaps even more important, is freeing ourselves from either blindly following, or reactively opposing, what our parents taught us is the "right" answer to this question. The influence of parents and other significant childhood figures may have been direct and verbal, but more often it was subtle and indirect, perceived in their behavior.

Next, I suggest looking at the various reasons we might have for wanting more than a modest level of wealth. Some of these are listed above and you may be aware of others that operate for you. How important does each of these seem—not generally but to you personally? Pondering these, and giving some sort of weighing to each, can move you appreciably toward a clearer awareness of the level of affluence that is appropriate for you.

It's also useful to imagine how your life might change if you raised, or lowered, your financial goals. How would you use additional money, and how would this affect you and others? Or, if you chose to allow more time for other pursuits, what would these be and how would this change your life and state of being? You might even experiment with exercises where you imagine what a day, a month, or a year would be like for you with more, or with less, wealth and the accompanying changes in how you spend your time.

As you engage in the process of choosing your financial goals, you will certainly want to include your spouse or other life partner, and possibly your children and others close to you. Much of this sort of searching is a solitary task, but decisions that follow are not solely yours.

Consulting with wise and experienced authorities can be very helpful in this process. Financial planners, especially when they know you, can play very useful roles. They can help you become clearer about your factual situation—e.g., what it is costing you to live now, what are some current expenses which may have dubious value for you, and how secure the financial future is for you and your family. They can also facilitate your searching process by asking questions, sharing their experience, and generally being supportive of your quest to find your own answer to this question.

Psychotherapy can be a most valuable adjunct to the process of discovering your own choice as to how much is enough. Good therapists help people in many ways, and one of the most useful is in guiding and support-ing their inward searching. The therapist won't give you answers, but he or she can serve an invaluable function in facilitating your own quest for your deepest personal values and priorities.

In choosing how much money is enough for you, it's important to keep in mind that this is for now, and that you will want to re-examine your decision from time to time. While it's true that some choices are somewhat irrevocable—like changing vocations—many are not. Recognizing that we are choosing for now, and not for eternity, makes the decision-making pro-cess a bit easier. You can keep in mind that, from time to time, you may want to reconsider your choice of your preferred level of affluence.

In conclusion, despite the crucial importance for us of our personal decision as to how much money is enough, most of us avoid or defer mak-ing this choice consciously. But determining the level of affluence that we intend for ourselves can greatly enhance the quality of our lives. And it's not as hard to do as we may fear.

CHAPTER 7
For Richer, For Poorer

One of our generally accepted cultural myths is that marrying into a fortune would be a major key to the good life. But many people discover, sadly and painfully, that life isn't always that easy. On the one hand, not everyone who marries into money finds life problem-free. On the other hand, many wealthy people who marry someone considerably less affluent also encounter difficulties. Indeed, the popular media seem to delight in reporting the problems that develop in relationships where the wealth of the two partners is substantially different. So, it appears that marrying into a fortune isn't the royal road to happiness, after all. Although many problems can plague such relationships, we also know that some couples seem to manage these situations well, to the benefit of all concerned. What is it that successful relationships do differently?

This chapter is intended to offer some guidance to people who have embarked or intend to embark on such a relationship, to parents whose children may do so, and to those who counsel them. I begin by pointing out some of the problems and pitfalls that are likely, and then shift the focus shifts toward solutions—ways of preventing difficulties, and handling those that do develop. The following examples are drawn from real situations I have encountered as a consultant; however, all identities are disguised.

The problems inherent in marriages where wealth is quite unequal are greatly influenced by attitudes: those brought in by each partner, by their parents, relatives and friends, and by social customs and opinions. Paradoxically, the belief that marrying into money is wonderful is frequently accompanied by negative judgments against those who do just this. Such condemnations are often based on envy. Further, marrying into wealth—like inheriting it—seems in conflict with the traditional American values that emphasize self-reliance and making one's own way. While the attitudes and judgments of others are inevitably significant, the more important issues have to do with each partner's own beliefs.

Clearly, attitudes toward such marriages are very different whether it is the man or the woman who has the wealth. This is partly a matter of cultural prejudices, but it's also archetypal—for thousands of generations men have been the providers and women the sustainers. Our culture is changing, of course, as women move into the work-place, but there are still strong biases against the man who marries a rich woman. For that reason, most of the examples that follow involve the more problematic situations, where the husband is the less wealthy partner.

The problems that accompany wealth differences are strongly exacerbated when there are considerable differences in levels of culture between the two—in education, manners, and social graces. Talking about "class" differences may not be politically correct, but there is a reality to it.

I observed a painful example of cultural difference when I worked with the Thompson family (not their real names), where the son, Henry, dated and finally married Frances, a young woman from a blue-collar background. Henry's parents, George and Helen, were appalled by their perception of the young woman's table manners, vocabulary, and obvious discomfort in social situations, especially with the parents' quite urbane friends. The parents saw Frances as the absolute antithesis of the wife they would have chosen for him. I urged them to accept this young woman as Henry's choice, and because of her very obvious caring and love for him and his for her. I also reminded them that Henry truly seemed to enjoy and to feel comfortable with their own group of friends, much more than with the people his parents would have chosen for him. They didn't see it this way, and couldn't or wouldn't truly accept her, although they seem to be making some progress in this regard. Overall, they simply could not understand that their son just did not want to live the sort of life, or to choose the friends and activities, they wanted for him. They felt hurt and betrayed by Henry, feeling he has rejected their values and therefore, they believe, rejected them.

These sorts of problems can be avoided or ameliorated when parents are willing to go through a graduation process. This means accepting the fact that they have essentially done all they can to help their children to grow and mature. Then their task is to welcome them as autonomous adults who can and will choose their own partners, careers, friends, and life styles. When parents are able to do this, they make a major contribution toward the happiness and freedom of all parties involved.

When significant wealth differences do exist, pre-marital or post-marital agreements are often encouraged. One reason such legal agreements are often advocated in wealthy families, by attorneys and by the wealthy parents is to minimize litigation. Parents, reasonably enough, are often concerned with the loss of their child's fortune in the case of divorce. They may also be aware of the likely complications should the divorce be followed by another marriage, particularly where children and stepchildren are involved.

More often than not, however, the young couple—in love and contemplating a life together—truly don't want to consider the possibility that their marriage might end. They can scarcely imagine, and don't want to consider, that their relationship could deteriorate to the point where fighting, even litigation over money, might occur.

Whether such legal agreements are wise and appropriate is a very individual matter. I have occasionally counseled young couples to decide what the agreement should entail and to do it together, particularly when having one seems quite important to the wealthier parents. But there have been some cases where it seemed that the damage to the trust in the relationship that often accompanies this process outweighed the advantages of the agreement. The couple needed to value their personal alliance over their wealth.

If the young people are considering such a contract, it's essential to the success of the arrangement that they both participate in the process and that they reach substantial agreement concerning the documents they sign. These arrangements are most damaging when the attorneys or the parents impose an agreement on a reluctantly compliant couple, who feel coerced.

A difficult problem for many young men contemplating marriage to a wealthy woman is facing the fact that any income they are going to contribute is going to be essentially irrelevant with regard to their security or standard of living. Some then feel that they are simply not going to be able to give their wife anything that she doesn't already have, or can easily get for herself. This can be damaging to a man's self-esteem and sense of his own manhood. Of course, it also makes it more difficult for a wealthy young woman to find a good partner.

When the daughter of the affluent parents in the King family chose a husband without wealth, they decided to gift the young man with a million dollars. This kind of gift can help to reduce the problems that accompany a partnership of financial inequality. As this arrangement seems to have worked to the satisfaction of all involved, I've occasionally recommended a similar solution to other wealthy parents. For such a gift to have the desired effect, it needs to develop out of open conversations with the two young people.

When children come into the picture it becomes even more important that parents handle money matters well. It can be quite damaging if the children see their father or mother as a parasite, lazy, living off their wealthy partner. They also need to be spared the experience of frequent or excessive parental conflicts about how money is spent or otherwise distributed. Another harmful experience for children is when a partner routinely defers to the wealthy one on money issues.

These problems are almost inevitably exacerbated by the baggage carried by the affluent partner, particularly if the wealth is inherited. Both sexes—but young women particularly—have been taught to be suspicious of anyone, especially a potential partner, and to always question their motives. One wealthy young man who had experienced a number of failed relationships told me: "I'm never sure whether they love me or it."

A central element in every good marriage is open discussion of all issues, and most especially those involving money. Studies have shown money to be the most frequent source of disputes in all marriages. Open discussion is, of course, particularly important for surmounting problems where major wealth discrepancies exist. In my observations, those couples who deal successfully with unequal wealth talk openly, and rather often, about money issues, before and during their marriage. This is especially crucial for decisions regarding investing and major expenditures or distributions. A useful principle is to avoid major unilateral decisions, since these inevitably result in resentment if not outright conflict. An exception can be where the partners agree openly that one of them is authorized to make certain financial decisions.

In addition to discussing issues, it's essential that the feelings of both partners be shared currently, openly and candidly. A key to doing this successfully is not waiting too long to deal with uncomfortable feelings—like anxiety, anger or hurt—and allowing them to become even more intense and difficult. Where the conflicts seem major and the feelings of either partner are intense, it can be useful to bring in a trained and neutral facilitator.

In a marriage that is fiscally unequal, both partners are almost certain to be troubled with conflicted, complex and ambivalent feelings. For instance, a non-wealthy husband is likely to enjoy the comforts and security that his wife's fortune provides, while at the same time feeling embarrassed, ashamed, even a bit guilty about her supporting him. And the wife, while pleased to be able to help him to have what he wants, is likely also to be plagued by unwanted suspicions, perhaps even some contempt for his living off her resources. Such emotions are most uncomfortable to live with and difficult to acknowledge. But couples usually find that having the courage and trust to share these feelings and attitudes with each other, strengthens their relationship.

It helps if both recognize that it's essentially inevitable that both partners will, at times, feel uncomfortable concerning ways that money is spent, how it's invested, who pays for what, how much is saved, and how it will be passed on after their death. It is generally helpful to accept that such feelings are quite normal and don't mean that they're selfish or greedy or lazy.

The general principle here is that a financially unequal relationship can probably be successful as long as both parties truly want it to succeed and are willing to work at it, and can reach, and maintain agreement, on significant issues. The couple needs to strive for accord on all questions having to do with money—where it comes from and how it's used. If they can maintain reasonable agreements and can be conscious and accepting of the issues where they differ, it will probably work; if they don't, it probably won't.

One common source of difficulties is the standard of living that they choose. In most marriages, regardless of the level of wealth, there are likely to be differences regarding the proportion of money spent to that saved. Regardless of the level of affluence, one partner is likely to be more inclined to enjoy whatever wealth they have, while the other will be more future-oriented and inclined to save. Couples need to recognize that this is not an uncommon situation, discuss it openly, and arrive at compromises that respect both of their attitudes.

In situations where the wife's assets make it optional for the husband to work for money, it's important that she respect (even if she does not agree with) what he chooses as his vocation—whether it's earning a great deal of money on his own, investing hers, starting a business, involving himself with non-profit organizations dedicated toward a better world, doing research, working in the arts, or whatever. My observation has been that without this kind of respect, the couples haven't much of a chance. If she can't fully support his vocational choice, this calls for considerable open dialogue, which ideally will lead either to a change in his occupation or in her attitude.

Some couples I've worked with have dealt with these tricky issues quite successfully, as indicated in the following examples:

The Andrews live on Helen's trust income, while Bob works with her on shared philanthropic and other projects. They've agreed on this partly to ensure their having plenty of time for good relationships with their children. Each is strongly committed to doing what they can toward creating a better world, and they thoroughly appreciate the opportunities to collaborate in work about which they care deeply.

Tom is a writer, seriously engaged in a career that doesn't bring in much income. Liz supports his vocation, both financially and emotionally, and this seems to be working out happily for both.

Joan and Bill share a passionate interest in the environment and are deeply involved, both with their money and much of their time, in a non-profit organization that supports and implements their hopes and ideals. Their work with this organization has provided them with friends and acquaintances with whom they share a great deal and whose companionship they thoroughly enjoy.

After some exploration of various career options, the Farnsworths have arrived at an arrangement by which Charles spends much of his time handling Rachel's trusts and investments. This is working for both; he enjoys and is good at this occupation and she's happy to be relieved of responsibilities that she finds boring. Their arrangement frees her to spend much time with their three children, her friends, and her philanthropic activities. This is an arrangement that at first made Rachel's parents and siblings quite uncomfortable and openly critical. But, since Charles is doing a good job with the money and the arrangement seems to be working well for everyone, the criticism has subsided.

John Bell manages Virginia's family's foundation. This is a full-time job that no direct family members wanted, and they all seem quite happy about it, largely because he does it responsibly and in accordance with their values.

In what I've found to be a rather common situation, Hal Johnson decided that he needed to earn enough to pay all of their not-inconsiderable expenses, and that Florence's trusts should be left intact to grow. He entered a career with a software company that seemed to require twelve-hour work days. After a while the couple realized that this arrangement was not good for either of them or their marriage, and it was particularly unfortunate for their two children. As an outcome of some months of discussion, they agreed to share all their expenses, with her trust paying half. This enabled him to shift his job and to create a more balanced life. The new arrangement appears to be working for everyone because it seems more equitable, it benefits all parties, and was arrived at through genuine agreement.

As I hope all this makes clear, there are all sorts of real and potential problems inherent in a marriage where there is a significant difference in the wealth that each partner brings. These difficulties stem largely from the beliefs and attitudes of the couple themselves, of their parents, other relatives and friends, and the society at large. But, as we keep leaning from the many couples who manage such situations well and happily, these are not insoluble problems.

In conclusion, couples that deal successfully with significantly unequal wealth usually live with these principles:

• They discuss, promptly and openly, all issues having to do with wealth, and with particular attention to the feelings involved.

• They encourage their parents to accept them as autonomous adults.

• They find shared interests and commitments—particularly those related to the wealth—such as philanthropic giving, being of service, their standard of living, and raising children.

CHAPTER 8
Power in the Family Business: Its Uses and Misuses

This chapter is intended to provide a clearer understanding of power, particularly as it is exercised in connection with the three key elements of a family business—the wealth, the family, and the business itself. It will become clear that power is a central force that works through these three elements of a family business and that ties them together. Therefore, the success of a family enterprise depends on the wise and appropriate use of power. The ways in which that power is exercised determine how the family serves its members; how the business serves the family, employees, and other constituents; how wealth is garnered and used; and even whether all three elements survive.

The central purpose of this essay is to explore ways in which power can be used effectively, so as to further the shared aims of all involved—to benefit the family and the business and to enable the wealth to serve both. The paper also shows how the inappropriate use of power is detrimental to all concerned.

The stories that are used here are essentially composites of what has actually happened in several families and family businesses. They are events that I have observed, been told of, or read about. (Naturally all names and other identifying data have been altered to prevent recognition of those involved.) All of the following stories illustrate the misuse of power—the first focusing on power within the family, the second on its misuse in the business, and the third on the wealth. Of course, all of these are interrelated, so that how power is used in one arena has effects in the others.

POWER MISUSED

Charles Thompson's father founded Wilmington Steel, a profitable medium-sized metal-fabricating business in Delaware. Charles took over the operation on his father's death and, combining his talents and dedication with a bit of luck, expanded it to a large, publicly-traded corporation. Charles was a hard-driving businessman, respected by most, feared by many, and loved by none.

He "managed" his wife and children much as he ran his business. Standards of achievement and behavior were high, and discipline was arbitrary and strict. When Malcolm, his eldest son, was ready to enter college, he told his father that he planned a pre-med major in order to move toward his deeply-desired goal of a career as a physician. Charles had never discussed Malcolm's education or his life goals with him, and Malcolm had been too intimidated to bring up such topics. The father was shocked and disappointed by this news, and he expressed his dissatisfaction by telling Malcolm that a medical career was out of the question. He explained that the eldest son's place was in the family business and that the young man would major in business in order to work in, and eventually take over, the family enterprise. This was clearly an instruction, not a suggestion, and Malcolm never considered questioning such a directive.

Charles's eighteen-year old daughter, Emily, was strongly interested in business and appeared to have considerable talents. She had hoped to find a career in the company with open-ended opportunities for advancement. But Charles dealt with her in the same manner as he had with Malcolm, telling her that as a young woman it was not appropriate for her to think of being a business executive and that she could never expect to do man's work as well as a man could. He even suggested that she might find a place as a secretary to one of her brothers in the business.

Harsh and arbitrary as these decisions seem, Charles truly believed that it was to everyone's benefit that the oldest son assume responsibility. for the company. He also believed that for a woman to become an executive would be bad for both the organization and for her. Charles was convinced that he was making decisions that were right for the company and for his children.

Malcolm did go to work in the business, eventually becoming CEO as planned. He worked hard, trying to deny his discomfort and unhappiness with his career and to putting out of his mind his dreams of the world of medicine. However, he lacked many of the personal qualities required of a good manager. These shortcomings, together with his joylessness and lack of enthusiasm in his work, resulted in his falling short of meeting the challenges the business came to face.

By the time the company was sold, the worth of the shares had dropped severely, Malcolm's siblings and their children were confronted with sharply reduced income, and relations between them became irrevocably strained. Malcolm has since lived with a deep sense of personal failure that has seriously damaged his sense of his own worth, as well as his relations with his wife and children. And Emily, the passed-over daughter, settled for a career that was never challenging and which she left to enter a less-than-satisfying marriage.

Henry Williams didn't have time to go to college and joined a real estate firm in California. He was a natural salesman, and he learned quickly, soon becoming a partner. One thing that Henry grasped was that buying and selling property was much more lucrative than dealing for commissions, so he started his own company to do just that. His capacity for taking risks, his intelligence, energy and judgment, and his willingness to work long hours combined to produce success, and Williams Realty soon became a large and profitable enterprise.

Like Charles Thompson, Henry Williams let his two daughters and two sons know that they were expected to work in the family business and, as they grew up, they did so. It was generally understood (although never stated) that one of them would eventually take Henry's place, if he were to retire or die (he didn't really expect either of these to happen). But Henry would never discuss this or allow his children or anyone to bring up the topic. When his wife or colleagues had the temerity to question him about succession, he simply said that it was good for his children not to know who would inherit the top position and that he would make this decision in his own good time. Not knowing their future would keep them working hard and prevent their becoming too secure and complacent. Henry had no question as to the validity of this proposition, and he delighted in citing examples to demonstrate its truth.

The Williams children participated in the firm as junior executives, in jobs that required them to work very hard but which did not permit them to learn much about how the enterprise was managed. The company's Board of Directors consisted entirely of family members and employees and seemed to exist only to satisfy legal requirements, since no substantive decisions were ever placed before the Board. Henry refused suggestions that capable and knowledgeable outside Board members be brought in, making it clear that he knew how to run the company much better than any fancy outside experts.

One day, to Henry's great surprise, he suffered cardiac arrest and died, leaving his little empire in disarray. None of the children felt competent to take over leadership, nor would they accept direction from any of their siblings. In this atmosphere of confusion, fear and anger, Margaret, Henry's widow, tried to mediate among her children to reach some acceptable agreement, but she was unable to do so. The situation kept deteriorating until finally one of the sons brought suit against his mother and brother and sisters. This was more than the now-fragile enterprise could bear, and the only answer was bankruptcy and forced sale of the company—at a very low price.

Peter and Frances Anderson built Computer Peripherals, a successful electronics firm in New England, and eventually their three children went to work in the company. The business produced substantial income, but the parents kept their children at low salaries, and the profits were reinvested in the business. Frances and Peter's motives were thoroughly honorable—they believed that if the children received too much money while they were relatively young—income which they hadn't truly earned—it would diminish their motivation and weaken their characters. For similar reasons Peter and Frances steadfastly refused to reveal to their children any information about the nature and size of the family estate or the parents' plans for its distribution. And, since they didn't want the children to see themselves as wealthy, they chose not to train them in the management of money.

As is so often the case, Peter and Frances were unaware of the effects of this withholding on their children. All were pained by what they saw as their parents' mistrust and lack of respect for them and, feeling not valued, kept them from having a healthy sense of their own worth. They were angry that they were treated in this way, although they never felt justified or safe in bringing this up with their parents.

When Peter and Frances died, most of their assets were divided among the three offspring. The young people then discovered that their parents, still suspicious of the harmful effects of spendable wealth, were maintaining their control from the grave. They did this by keeping all of the assets, except for the company, under the management of a bank trust department, with very little income to go to the beneficiaries during their lifetimes.

The three heirs did take over management of the family business. Because their incomes from the bank were so small and they were so inadequately prepared, and because they were angry at how they'd been treated, they managed the business so as to bring in very substantial income to themselves. This worked for a short time, but eventually the business could no longer survive this sort of management and cash outflow. It began a downhill slide that ended in bankruptcy. This failure led to considerable pain and strife among the children, and relationships among them have never recovered.

Each of these stories illustrates how power can be destructive. Charles Thompson of the steel-fabricating company misused his power in the family. Henry Williams abused his in his real estate business. And the Andersons used poor judgment in the way they employed the power of their wealth. In each case, considerable damage resulted—to the business, the family, and the wealth. And, in each case, it didn't have to be that way.

All of these parents behaved as they did for what they sincerely believed were decent and honorable motives. This was not a matter of bad people doing bad things. All of the parents wanted the family business to continue after them, and they wanted their children to participate in its future. The problems that they created weren't a result of malevolence but of ignorance and bad judgment. This is usually the case when a family business doesn't survive the transfer to the next generation and doesn't work out to the benefit of those involved. These cases also illustrate the damage that can be done unwittingly by people with an excessive personal need for power.

POWER DEFINED

Among the definitions of power in *Webster's New Collegiate Dictionary* are "possession of control, authority or influence over others" and "ability to act or produce an effect." Interestingly, for the topic of this paper, another of Webster's definitions identifies power as "a source or means of supplying energy." Jeffrey Pfeffer, in his book, *Managing With Power: Politics and Influence in Organizations*, says, "Power is the potential ability to influence behavior, to change the course of events, to overcome resistance, and to get people to do things that they would not otherwise do."

Power can come from one's position (CEO, parent), and it can result from being perceived as having special knowledge and talents. The ability to be granted power can also be an element of the personality; there are charismatic people who emanate power and tend to get their way (a theme that will be discussed later in the chapter).

Having power often implies being able to enforce one's wishes where the acceptance or refusal of what is desired has consequences, positive or negative. This could be overt ("Do this or you're fired") or more subtle ("Do this or I won't respect or love you"). Even more subtle is, "If you don't do this I'll feel badly," or "My careful plans, into which I've put so much, will be ruined." And those in positions of power—in the family or in business—may send out ambivalent messages, such as "Do this and sometimes I will respect and love you and at other times I will withhold my response."

Power is a central reality in life—perhaps nowhere more so than in a family enterprise. Where family members are in business together, power is the factor that runs through, and across, all of the elements—within the family, in the conduct of the business, and in the management and distribution of the wealth. Yet, power is often overlooked, unexamined, and unrecognized. The implicit taboo against talking about power directly and openly is similar to those having to do with sex and wealth; and I believe it is just as destructive. Each of these taboos is harmful to the family unit and to the individuals in it, and the taboo against discussing power is damaging to the business as well.

Jeffrey Pfeffer, in discussing the apparent decline of American business, says: "If leadership involves skill at developing and exercising power and influence as well as the will to do so, then perhaps one of the causes of the so-called leadership crisis in organizations in the United States is the attempt to sidestep issues of power. Unless and until we are willing to come to terms with organizational power and influence, and admit that the skills of getting things done are as important as the skills of figuring out what to do, our organizations will fall farther and farther behind." What Pfeffer might have said is that this is a uniquely American problem because of our myth of being a democratic, classless society, in which all are equal.

Power itself, of course, is neither positive nor negative. Just as electrical power can be used to light rooms or to electrocute people, interpersonal power can serve its users and those affected by it, or it can be damaging to one or all of those involved. Commenting on Lord Acton's famous dictum about the corrupting nature of power, George Bernard Shaw said: "Power does not corrupt men, but fools, if they get into a position of power, corrupt power." Perhaps this is a typical Shaw overstatement—power often does corrupt. Still, it is an idea worth considering.

The use of power in business is usually, but by no means always, rather direct and clear. With wealth it is less so, especially where parents use the money and its current and planned distribution to manipulate their children to behave as desired. Power within the family is usually a much more subtle and complex matter. This is particularly true as the children grow through adolescence to adulthood, when they resist the power of their parents and claim their own.

Power can bring freedom, and this is one of the reasons it is so zealously pursued. Being empowered means having choice, being able to select among options and to live out what was chosen. Power can bring freedom from unwelcome demands and restrictions, and it can provide freedom to pursue attractive options in life. Karl Deutsch has pointed out that holding power can free people from the need to keep learning—that people often seek power in order to control their environment so that they can limit change and unknowns and no longer need to keep learning.

But power can also limit freedom, particularly where the power is more than can be handled well. Being in a position of authority, whether in the company or the family, brings responsibilities, which are usually restrictive. Also, maintaining this position can require careful attention to one's actions and behavior, which can be a serious limitation of freedom.

The much discussed "loneliness at the top" characterizes the sense people in power often have of being without peers and unable to discuss their concerns freely. But Manfred F. R. Kets de Vries, in his book, *Prisoners of Leadership*, suggests that this loneliness may be a platitude and an illusion. "Actually it may be better to speak of the loneliness of command in the context of isolation from reality. The inability to test our perceptions, the tendency to lose touch with reality, is a danger anyone can fall victim to when in a position of leadership." Maintaining "reality" through selective perception is one way of being corrupted by power.

One of the principal sources of misuse of power is simple greed, perhaps tinged with vanity—craving power for its own sake and for its apparent ability to feed self-esteem. It may be that anyone who really wants power probably shouldn't have very much of it. After some study of organizations and their management, the noted psychologist, Abraham Maslow, wrote: "The person who seeks for power is the one who is just exactly likely to be the one who shouldn't have it, because he neurotically and compulsively needs power. Such people are apt to use power very badly; that is, use it for overcoming, overpowering, hurting people, or, to say it in other words, they use it for their own selfish gratifications, conscious and unconscious, neurotic as well as healthy.... The safest person to give power to is the one who doesn't enjoy power. He is the least likely to use it for selfish, neurotic or sadistic purposes ... If a person struggles for leadership and for bosshood, then this is one dangerous point against him that should make us question his ability". And Thomas Jefferson wrote "I have never been able to conceive how any rational being could propose happiness to himself from the exercise of power over others."

The possession and the use of power offer powerful and seductive ego rewards, and these can easily become addictive. Power can be as habituating as alcohol or any other drug, and the harmful effects of such addiction are likely to be at least as destructive, though often less obvious. One-time U.S. Secretary of State James Byrnes wrote: "Power intoxicates men. When a man is intoxicated by alcohol, he can recover, but when intoxicated by power, he seldom recovers." And in the eighteenth century the British statesman and author, Edmund Burke, wrote: "Those who have once been intoxicated with power, and have derived any kind of emolument from it, even though but for one year, can never willingly abandon it." Strong statements, but worth considering, given the sources.

It's often difficult to see the difference between someone wanting power in order to accomplish certain objectives, and just desiring it for its own sake. But the difference in outcomes is impressive. Power directed toward objectives, such as the welfare of the family or the business, is likely to achieve those goals, to benefit the activity and the people for which the power is used. Power exercised for the gratification of the one holding it may or may not achieve that goal, but, sooner or later, such use of power is almost certain to damage the organization and those involved. And it often turns out that the person who uses power for selfish motives suffers from this in the long run.

Any misuse of power is likely to be damaging to all concerned—to the organization, to those subject to the power, and to the person who is misusing his or her power. But probably even more damage is done in the process of the transition of power than in the use of it. Shifts of power—within the family, in the business, and in the management and distribution of the wealth—are usually sensitive and precarious processes, minefields of hurt feelings, resentments, destructive ignorance, and just plain mismanagement. A discussion of the transmission of power later in this chapter will comment on how, and why, this is true and on what can be done toward constructive transitions.

THE USES OF POWER IN BUSINESS, FAMILY AND WEALTH

POWER IN THE BUSINESS

The need for structure, control, and clearly-defined authority, is generally recognized and accepted in most enterprises. When this tacit agreement is misused or exploited, trouble ensues. Still, the need for and the use of power in business are usually accepted without too much difficulty, certainly as compared to power in the family and with wealth.

A crucial and central focus of power in the family business has to do with succession. As we saw with Henry Williams's real estate company, the question of who will take over the power as the father/CEO withdraws can overwhelm the company and the family. If this element of power is not recognized and dealt with openly beforehand, the seeds are sown for struggles that will be damaging to the business and to the family.

Family businesses often fail to deal wisely with succession because the CEO will not confront his eventual loss of power through aging and death. In working with these men, I've noted how often, when they have to discuss such matters, they will say "if something happens to me..." This is not just euphemistic; it betrays their inability and unwillingness to confront the reality of their mortality—that they are impermanent. While almost all of us find it difficult to face up to disability and death, being powerful makes it considerably more of a problem.

Difficulties in a family business can stem from the arbitrary assignment of power to family members. In many family businesses, children or other relatives of the CEO are given stature and authority well beyond their talents and experience in order to prepare them for eventual succession to leadership.

One of the most prevalent issues facing family-controlled businesses is maintaining good working relationships between family members in positions of authority and employees subordinate to them. The outside executives may be superior to the family members in experience and abilities and, even if they're not more talented than the family members, they're likely to believe that they are. Introducing family members into positions of authority is often resented by experienced and capable managers and employees, and the danger of losing the talents of these valued people, either outright or through lowered morale, must be dealt with.

Therefore, when family members enter and rise in the business, it is important that they exercise their power sensitively, judiciously, and with some humility. Insuring that this happens is a responsibility of the senior family member, as well as part of the training of young people who are being prepared for the business. A wise parent/CEO will be alert to behavior on the part of the young people that could be perceived as arrogant and insensitive, and he or she will move quickly and firmly to change this. A wise and respected avuncular figure, possibly but not necessarily a family member, can usually serve this function even more effectively than can the CEO.

In order not to lose valuable employees, it is also important to maintain clear, honest, and open communication with them as to their prospects. They need to know which positions in the firm are potentially available to them and which are likely to be filled by family members.

As will be discussed more fully in the next section, problems can develop in family-controlled businesses when power relationships within the family carry over into the business, usually unconsciously. When this happens, the use and acceptance of power become unclear; and confusion, resentments and struggles can be expected.

The father who is head of the household may inappropriately transfer this authority to his role in the business. A father who has grown accustomed to dominating his family, to making decisions that seem to be accepted without challenge, may well continue such autocratic behavior in the business, with unhappy results. And a father who finds his wife and children rejecting his authority may attempt to compensate for this by becoming a tyrant in the office where, unlike the situation at home, he has the authority to force people to obey.

Sons or daughters who feel impotent within the family are usually unable to accept responsibilities in the company. If they've grown up without an adequate sense of self-esteem, they will lack confidence in themselves or their abilities. This is likely to cause them to avoid hard decisions and to fail to exercise their appropriate authority. But sometimes young people who feel impotent at home may attempt to compensate by going to the other extreme and trying to exert power beyond their role or their capacities within the organization.

Struggles among family members can lead to other problems with power in the business because of the carryover of family relationships. These often are a continuation of sibling rivalries that have developed in the family, as well as long-standing authority conflicts between parents and children.

A 1976 article, "Transferring Power in the Family Business," by Louis B. Barnes and Simon A. Hershon, in the *Harvard Business Review*, deals with many of these issues. The authors consider four groups of people concerned with the business—those inside the family: the family managers and the relatives—and those outside the family: the employees and the outsiders. They go on to say: "A curious irony is that the more 'outside' the family the perspective is ... the more legitimate it seems as a 'real' management problem... These inside the family problems tend to be ignored in management books, consultants' reports, and business school courses. Ignoring these realities can be disastrous for both the family and the company." In the last few years particularly, power struggles have become likely where daughters are treated by their parents as inferior to sons and are given less authority. This used to be considered normal and acceptable (at least by the men). But recently fathers who attempt to bypass their daughters in allocating power are finding that this can lead to difficult challenges and battles—or a painful sense of rejection by dutiful and loving daughters who cannot understand or accept their fathers' sexist attitudes.

POWER IN THE FAMILY

The use of power within the family, particularly where the members are in business together, is usually more complex and subtle than is power in the business itself. In order to gain some comprehension of the intricacies of relationships within the family, knowledge of "family systems theory" is recommended. A discussion of this way of viewing the dynamics within the family is beyond the scope of this paper. However, there are a number of good books on family systems theory; one of the most-respected is *Turning Point*, by Frank Pitman, M.D.

From infancy, when parents have nearly total power over their children, begins a process of relinquishing authority, until, at last, children and parents can regard each other as equals, in "eye-level" relationships. But this is a process that is often aborted by parents who are unwilling to let go, and by children who are reluctant to accept the responsibilities of independence.

The progress of the children from dependency to independence is absolutely crucial for their well-being and for there to be a "functional" family. This is particularly true when the family owns a business that the children will enter and move into positions of power. When an enterprise is managed by family members, interdependence is required for the health of the business, the family, and the individuals involved. This means that truly independent, autonomous individuals freely choose to be together and to work cooperatively in ways that acknowledge that they need each other. An attitude of interdependence is a prerequisite for an effective leadership team, whether or not they are family members. But the need is even greater when the leaders are related, and the challenges of achieving this are like-wise greater.

Another aspect of power within the family that is fraught with problems and possibilities is in the relationship between the parents. When the father dominates the mother, often by using the power of his position and his wealth, this way of relating is not only bad for them and their marriage, but it sends a detrimental message to the children. If the parents don't demonstrate interdependency, it's hard for the children to value and to achieve for themselves this way of being, which is so essential in a family business. This is particularly true for daughters, who are likely to grow up within the old cultural stereotypes about women's place. Whether they submit to this or rebel, the results are likely to be costly for all.

In many families, especially if they are in business, the father—particularly if he is the entrepreneur who built the business—holds and exercises overt power over his wife and his children, much as he does at work. But, looking beneath the surface, we often find that the wife has established and maintains her own power, covertly and subtly. Somehow it seems that life decisions involving the children and the family tend to go the way she wishes, although this is a fact that may never be recognized or acknowledged. And her role and her power as mediator of conflicts between the father and his sons and daughters, and among the siblings, is often legendary.

Also, it's important not to overlook the power of the children that, like that of the mother, is likely to be subtle, covert, and unrecognized. Young people are usually wiser and more observant than their parents (particularly their father) realize, and the children may become expert at getting their way. The more autocratic the father, the wilier will be the children at achieving power. Young ones quickly learn of their parents' need for their respect and affection, and their concern with guilt, and children may become surprisingly adroit at offering or withholding approval and affection to manipulate their parents.

In considering the power of wives and children, it's worth noting that one seldom-recognized way of achieving and holding power is to be perceived as weak and helpless. In families, and even in businesses, it can be surprisingly enlightening to watch people with overt power protect and cater to the "weak" ones. While those involved would hardly dare to suggest that the appearance of weakness is being used manipulatively, it often seems to turn out that way.

THE POWER OF WEALTH

Wealth brings power, and power is used in acquiring and managing wealth. As individuals accumulate more and more assets, at some point their motivation is likely to shift from wanting the money as a way of providing comfort and security for themselves and their families, to desiring it for its own sake. The wish to possess substantial wealth may be for competitive and status reasons ("He who dies with the most toys wins"), and it may be because the game itself is exciting and gratifying, often more so than any other activity the person can imagine. But, people often continue to strive to accumulate more and more because of the power wealth conveys. Wealth can be used to establish control over people, including one's own family members. And investing money can give affluent people power to help create social and economic conditions that they desire (and may not necessarily be what others in the family consider desirable).

One use of the power of wealth, which is often controversial within the business family, has to do with ongoing decisions such as re-investing profits back into the enterprise versus distributing them to family members and other shareholders. Peter and Frances Anderson chose to keep re-investing the profits in their electronics business, and they decided this unilaterally, without considering the wishes of their children. Later the children, when they got the power, made the opposite decision, which turned out to be even more destructive.

Parents may use the power of their wealth to control their children in ways that can be harmful to everyone. Often there is a threat, usually tacit, that the children's inheritance is dependent on their living according to their parents' wishes. While this is usually rationalized as wanting the best for the younger people, it is often not received as such and can lead to great resentment. Even worse, being controlled this way by parents inhibits the process of developing healthy self-esteem and independence. The damage that this excessive control can do is particularly evident when the control continues well after the children have passed their formative years, as it often does.

A sign of misuse of the power of wealth within the family is unwillingness of parents to discuss it, so that the children are taught, subtly, that the topic is not acceptable. Refusal by parents to discuss any subject serves as a message to the children that there's something wrong with that topic and, more seriously, that their parents don't trust them.

The prevalent taboo against talking about wealth is one of the stranger superstitions in our culture—and a destructive one, especially within the family. The word "taboo" refers to certain behaviors that are forbidden within the society. The "civilized" world has its own set of taboos with sex being the most obvious. But just as "nice" people don't talk about sex, an antipathy to talking about personal wealth pervades our culture. While a number of reasons are cited for this prohibition, none of them account for the prevalence or the intensity of this taboo.

Many affluent parents keep the younger generation in the dark about the nature and the size of the family wealth and about how the estate will be distributed. While their conscious motives are usually benign, the effects on the children are destructive. More often than not, the parents' true motives are not expressed (and often are not conscious), as they have to do with the power over their children that the parents hold by being secretive. Also, parents are often fearful of opening up conflict with their children and dealing with their rebellion and rage. When the sons and daughters don't know much about the family wealth or their inheritance, it tends to keep them dependent on their parents and unempowered.

HOW TO USE POWER APPROPRIATELY

Theodore Roosevelt said: "Power undirected by high purpose spells calamity; and high purpose by itself is utterly useless if the power to put it into effect is lacking."

Recognizing how the improper use of power is counterproductive, it's time to consider its effective use. There are several principles that can be followed toward the appropriate exercise of power. Each of these is rather simple to understand, but many are difficult to put into effect. The following section will look at some of these in order to gain more understanding of ways that power can be used productively, and to become more aware of the barriers that can interfere with putting these into practice.

PLACE POWER IN THE HANDS OF THOSE
WHO CAN USE IT WELL

Manfred F. R. Kets de Vries, in his very useful book, *Prisoners of Leadership*, discusses in considerable depth the personal qualities that tend to bring people into positions of power, that make for effective leadership, and the traits that cause some leaders to use their power to the detriment of their organizations and themselves. Much in his book is of particular significance to family enterprises, since he explores characteristics common to many leaders.

As has been noted by other observers, de Vries discusses differences between entrepreneurs and managers—a distinction of particular importance when control of a family company passes from its founder to his or her successor. Personal traits that are likely to be present in someone who creates an enterprise are often not suitable—and may even be counterproductive—once the business is well under way. F. Derek du Toit wrote in a 1980 article in the *Harvard Business Review*, "Confessions of a Successful Entrepreneur," that "the entrepreneur who starts his own business generally does so because he is a difficult employee. He does not take kindly to suggestions or orders from other people... once the business gets larger, requiring the support and active cooperation of more people, he is at risk if he does not change his approach. It has been correctly stated that the biggest burden a growing company faces is having a full-blooded entrepreneur as its owner."

Among the personal qualities which de Vries cites as common to many executives and potentially damaging when they are excessive, are: narcissism, aggressiveness, suspiciousness, being histrionic, detachment, controlling, passive-aggressiveness, dependency, and masochism. A discussion of these traits is not feasible or appropriate here, and the interested reader is encouraged to pursue these in de Vries' book.

He also discusses the powerful and elusive quality of charisma, often seen in entrepreneurs. A powerful asset in a leader, particularly for a new enterprise or one undergoing major changes, its shadow side can include attraction and development of middle-management people who are not adequately independent, forceful, or competent. Many highly competent people just don't want to work under such a leader.

Significantly for the family enterprise, de Vries suggests "if anyone can influence the entrepreneur's leadership style, it is usually an outsider. Someone not heavily exposed to the organization's culture has the greatest impact..." Extrapolating a bit, it suggests the importance of empowering outsiders, through board positions or as consultants, as a way of compensating for deficiencies in the leadership qualities of any person in power, entrepreneur or not.

USE POWER OPENLY

Power, whether in the family, the enterprise, or with wealth, should be understood and used knowledgeably. This means that those in power recognize how important it is that all those affected have a clear understanding of where the power lies and how it operates. As discussed, leaders may choose consciously to conceal and to distort their use of power, or they may be dri-ven by unconscious forces to keep members of their families, their employees, (and perhaps themselves), in the dark.

Those in authority need to be aware that their power will be more effective if its use is straightforward. Open use of power means that all questions regarding it are legitimate—that there are no secrets and no taboos. Paradoxically, allowing those affected by power to question its use is likely to strengthen those who are exercising the power. When those subject to authority feel free to question, even to challenge it, they are more likely to respect and accept it. Power used covertly and deceptively becomes negative in its effects, breeding confusion, misunderstandings, resentments, and resistance. When people obey unwillingly, they're apt to find ways, consciously or not, of resisting that power and of interfering with the achievement of the desired results.

USE POWER TO ACHIEVE SHARED OBJECTIVES

In whatever arena, power functions best—to the benefit of all—when its use is directed toward clearly-defined purposes, preferably shared by all involved. This sounds easy, but it means that the person with authority must be as conscious and mindful as possible regarding his or her motives, so as to minimize desire for self-aggrandizement or ego-gratification in any of its forms. Insuring that the CEO's purposes are, in fact, shared by those most involved requires open discussion among them, often with the help of an outside facilitator.

Achieving goals, whether related to the business, the wealth or the family, requires the use of power. Appropriate use of power, when focused on those goals, is likely to be effective. But, to the extent that power becomes an end in itself, it is almost certain to interfere with the achievement of the purposes for which it is ostensibly intended. It's hard to have it both ways: power can serve the family, the business and the wealth—or it can feed the ego of the empowered person.

TRY FOR ACCEPTABLE DECISIONS

Power works best when its use is accepted—"deriving its just powers from the consent of the governed" (from the Declaration of Independence of the United States). People in authority must strive to persuade those subject to their decisions that following is, indeed, in their best interests. To achieve this, the leader should involve those most affected in the decision-making process and, after it is made, make clear the nature of the decision and the reasons behind it. Decisions and orders that are perceived as arbitrary and irrational will be resisted, actively or subtly. And the leader must never forget that people are seldom convinced by logic and reason alone.

Of course, it doesn't always turn out that decisions made by the person in power are accepted. Sometimes the leader is unable to convince those subject to his/her judgments that what is being conveyed to them is to their advantage. In such cases, the person in power should first reconsider his or her directive, talking it over with those who will be most affected and who are resistant to accepting what is being proposed. If the decision still seems right, then it will probably need to be communicated as an order, but without any explicit or implicit threats. When the leader comes to a point where persuasion is no longer effective, the instruction, "Do this because I say so" (with an explanation that a decision must be made, even without consensus) is a much more effective than a direct or covert, "Do this or I'll punish you." And this is true whether dealing with business subordinates or one's offspring.

If people subject to the power are to accept it willingly, it's important that they view the person in authority as meriting the position that he or she holds. Ordinarily most people in a family or organization are reasonably ready to assume that the person(s) in power deserve the authority that goes with the position, whether parental or supervisory. But there are times when this prerogative is not accepted, in the business and in the family, and these represent challenges for those in authority. Having power demands continuous work toward personal excellence—to demonstrate, to oneself and to others—the appropriateness of one's position. Holding power is not easy, and those who are in that position must keep showing that they merit it—by their knowledge, their talents, and their wisdom.

It sometimes happens—in business, with wealth, and in the family— that a decision of the leader meets with such resistance that it is in everyone's best interests to take the time to work things out. This usually means sitting down together, perhaps for as long as it takes to reach a mutually acceptable agreement—one that everyone can live with. This sort of conflict resolution can take place even though it is understood that the person with the power—boss or parent—reserves the right to make the final decision and that it's not a fully democratic process. Yet, when issues are perceived as important and feelings run high, the willingness of the person in power to explain his or her point of view, to listen carefully to those affected, and to thoughtfully consider changing his/her decision, can go a long way toward the willing acceptance of a step that is opposed by some.

When tensions are high and trust low, it is worthwhile to bring in an outside, objective, mutually acceptable facilitator/mediator, preferably a professional and not someone associated with or dependent on the family or any of its members. As one who has served professionally in this capacity, I have found that the presence of a trusted facilitator/mediator can lower anxieties, make it easier for participants to express opinions and feelings that may be unwelcome, and increase confidence that a positive outcome is possible.

SEE THAT TRANSITIONS OF POWER SERVE ALL INTERESTS

There are many ways of shifting power badly—ways that do not serve the interests of those involved—and we read about these every day. Probably the principal, single cause of such errors is the unwillingness of the person with the power, usually the father/CEO, to relinquish it. Many people with power avoid dealing with the transition issue, putting it off for so long that, when it happens, it is likely to result in conflicts and mismanagement, as described in examples at the beginning of this paper. The transition of power can also be aborted by unwillingness or lack of preparation of the younger generation, who may not want or know how to pick up the reins. Often young people, especially when their father is a hard-driving entrepreneur type, find power distasteful or frightening, and they try to avoid dealing with it. This can be fine if they choose another occupation where this isn't an issue, but if they stay in the family business, by choice or directive, it can spell disaster for them and for the business.

For transitions of power, especially between generations, to be successful, it's important that several conditions be in place:

Plans for the transition are understood by all involved

This usually means that the person(s) holding the power (CEO, parent) has opened up the topic, explained clearly to the family (spouse and children) his or her intentions, including the timetable when he or she intends to start retiring and how quickly the process will proceed. In a family company, it also implies that key non-family employees are kept informed of transition plans: when, how, and to whom the authority will shift.

Transition plans are open for reconsideration

Transitions usually proceed much more smoothly and painlessly when those affected have had opportunities to question—even to challenge them—and when the parent and/or CEO can truly listen to such ques-   tions. This not only contributes to clarity of understanding but, more importantly, it makes it more likely there will be "the consent of the governed." Furthermore, it often happens that questions and challenges regarding the leader's intentions contribute toward a better plan for succession and a more successful and trouble-free transition.

One important reason to open up these plans for discussion and possible modification is that it might turn out that the young person(s) selected for succession may not really desire the privilege or they may not be the best choice. That person may prefer a different career and could be temperamentally or intellectually poorly suited. Sometimes the person chosen doesn't want the responsibilities involved or feel adequate to handle them. In such a case, he or she may just need to be encouraged and trained. Or it may be that their self-judgment is accurate and that they are the wrong person for the job.

Those relinquishing power do so willingly

In most family business situations, of course, this is the stickiest and most troublesome issue. Especially with men or women who built their own companies, even thinking about letting go of the controls is likely to be avoided. When being powerful seems to be an essential part of one's identity, it's very hard to face its loss. Often, such people find it hard to believe that anyone, particularly their children, could ever manage their company properly. And, even if they might manage, certainly not yet. More subtly, considering succession issues requires facing up to mortality, to the reality that the parent/CEO is going to experience diminution of energy and powers, and, finally, death—the ultimate loss of power.

Many CEO's, especially entrepreneurs, have devoted so much of their lives to the business that they are quite unable to imagine the experience of retirement. When they do, they're likely to picture endless dismal days of golf and travel, and to be unable to imagine creative and satisfying pursuits after the business. This prospect is experienced ambivalently by most parents who manage companies. On the one hand, they are eager to have their child(ren) move ahead and take over the company. On the other hand, they are fearful of what this implies for their own lives.

Harry Levinson, in the *Harvard Business Review*, March-April 1971, says, "For the founder the business is an instrument, an extension of himself. So he has great difficulty giving up his baby, his mistress, his instrument, his source of social power, or whatever else the business may mean to him." He goes on to describe a situation where the father/CEO keeps holding on to his power: "Now, when John is middle-aged, he and his father are still battling. In effect John is asking, 'Why don't you let me grow up?' and his father is answering, 'I'm the only man around here. You must stay here and be my boy.'"

Manfred de Vries, discussing the various internal forces that interfere with leaders passing on their power, suggests: "When we hear CEO's commenting that they have no time to train a successor, or that, in spite of overwhelming evidence to the contrary, the succession problem has been taken care of, we can be sure that these psychological forces are at work."

It's helpful if the CEO can begin planning the transition of power well in advance of its actuality. Becoming conscious of one's ambivalence and its intensity is the first step in moving toward willingness to let go. Talking about it with one's spouse, friend, or a psychotherapist can be most helpful. Using help to plan an active and satisfying life after retirement—considering all the possibilities of challenging, enjoyable and useful pursuits—can provide a major step in moving toward willingness to let go. Also, becoming aware of the meaning and value of allowing one's children to develop in this way, and to find fulfillment for their own lives, can help to diminish fears and reluctance to relinquish power and position. Letting go can be done; for most leaders of family enterprises it's a difficult process—but a necessary one.

Barnes and Hershon, in their 1976 *Harvard Business Review* article, say: "Our studies suggest that the healthiest transitions are those old-versus-young struggles in which both the family managers and the business change patterns. For this to happen, 'the old man' must face the decision of helping the company live even though he must die. If he can do this, the management of transitions can begin. In effect, a successful transition can mean a new beginning for the company."

Productive retirement means learning new skills, a new way of being—a process full of exciting experiences, particularly for entrepreneurial types who thrive on challenge and innovation. Embarking on a new learning curve, where it's steep and progress is obvious, constitutes one of life's greatest pleasures, especially for people who enjoy innovation. Such a vision can help leaders to see retirement from the business more as the beginning of a new life than as the end of something.

Those succeeding are prepared for their responsibilities

Keeping those affected informed of transition plans helps in the process of training the ones succeeding to power, whether in the company, the family, or the management of the wealth. Many family enterprises do not survive the retirement or death of the founding entrepreneur because the members of the next generation are not adequately prepared to take over the responsibilities that devolve to them. Not only must they know that they will come into power and what their responsibilities will be, but they need to have a reasonable idea as to when this is likely to happen (more precise than the common, "if anything happens to me . . .")

It's important that whoever is holding the power work out a program of training for the daughters and sons who will assume responsibilities, teaching them the knowledge and the skills they will need. Some of this can be delegated (to business schools, professionals, consultants, other executives, et al) but much should come directly from their father and/or mother. It is particularly important that the children become clear about their parents' ways of understanding and using power. The apprentice system of training, in which the young person learns by doing, under wise and skilled supervision, is what works best for transmitting management skills.

In some family businesses, the heir apparent (including, of course, the heiress apparent) receives his or her initial training by working in another company, unrelated to the family, while in others, members of the younger generation move directly from school to positions in the family company, usually starting low on the ladder but moving up rather swiftly. There are advantages and disadvantages to both ways of preparing young people for responsibilities of leadership. Which way works better seems to depend on the individual situation and the nature of the key people involved.

It should be noted that some authorities question the wisdom of family members succeeding to power in the business at all. Harry Levinson, in his 1971 article in the *Harvard Business Review*, said "I know of no family business capable of sustaining regeneration over the long term solely through the medium of its own family members." and "In general, the wisest course for any business, family or non-family, is to move to professional management as quickly as possible." In my own experience this is much too broad a generalization. There are many exceptions.

The process of transition is respected

Periods of transition, for an individual or for an organization, are considerably more difficult and problematic than is usually recognized. We know something about the kinds of stresses that can accompany major life changes: marriage, divorce, moving, illness, losing a job or starting a new one. There's growing recognition that such life experiences are not simply a matter of finishing one thing and starting something new.

William Bridges consults with organizations going through transition processes. In his book *Surviving Corporate Transition*, he shows that when a major change takes place in personal or corporate lives, it entails three stages: The first is **The Ending**—recognizing that a stage in life is over and letting it go. Next is **The Neutral Zone**—an uncomfortable period of feeling lost, directionless, depressed and discouraged. Finally, comes **The Beginning**, when people, and organizations, finally begin to become aware of what's next for them and are able to make a new start. Many individuals and organizations try to abort this natural process, particularly to cut short the **Neutral Zone**, by prematurely grasping at something new, at great cost to the individual and to the organization.

Bridges points out that successful organizational transitions require that they allow time for the changes to take place, with awareness of their effects on the people in the organization. When leadership in a family passes from the parents to one or more of the children, a period of anxiety, confusion and stress can be expected. Recognizing this and allowing for it, with some faith that the process won't last forever, is critical to making the transition one that will serve everyone. The same is true when leadership in the business begins to shift from one generation to the next. This is likely to occasion confusion and stress, not only in the family members involved but also in other members of the organization. As with individual transitions, the key is consciousness. Being aware of what is happening, knowing that it's perfectly normal and that it is time-limited, and communicating this awareness to all involved—combine to reduce the discomfort and potential destructiveness of the traumas associated with transition. Essential to this process is bringing these issues and experiences out into the open, encouraging all involved to talk about what's happening—to the organization and to themselves. And executives should pay particular attention to the needs of the employees, assuring them that they are valued and that every effort will be made to ensure that they are not harmed by the transition.

Barnes and Hershon, in their previously cited article, say: "At some point a critical network of family managers, employees, relatives, and outsiders must begin to focus on the duality of both family and business transitions. Such talks should, in our opinion, begin at least 7 to 8 years before the president is supposed to retire. Even though the specific plans may change, the important assumptions behind those plans will not." Along with this goes a realization that they are all involved in a process, and that it will come to an end—that there is life after the transition.

The transition process is a complex and subtle one, often not well understood by those executives involved. Executives tend to focus on the outcomes of the transition—where the organization needs to go—while neglecting the crucial importance of the process. For this reason, outside consultants can provide a most valuable service in helping the organization move through its transition.

POWER USED PROPERLY

After exploring ways in which power can be used effectively and appropriately—so that it serves the interests of all—let's see how it can work. Here are the stories with which this paper began, retold on the assumption that those involved understood the effective use of power and operated accordingly:

Charles Thompson did not insist that his son forego his desired career in medicine in order to take over the family steel fabricating business. When he realized that Malcolm had other career aims, he understood that forcing him to work for the family company wouldn't be right for Malcolm or for the business. Charles voluntarily chose, in the best interests of all to forego using some of his power. He encouraged his son in his medical training and career, and Malcolm became a respected doctor and is living a satisfying life.

Because he knew his children well, Charles realized that his daughter, Emily, had a strong interest in business and specifically in the family enterprise. He encouraged her to apply to business school, which she completed and, after a few years in another business, joined the family company. Charles guided her learning and her progress through the company, and she developed into a fine executive. He made sure that it was understood, in the company and in the family, that Emily was the heiress apparent, and he worked behind the scenes to prepare key executives to accept a woman as their leader. He began reducing his active involvement in the business and found much satisfaction in becoming active in community and philanthropic activities. Emily took on more and more responsibility and authority. Eventually, she became president, and when Charles was ready for full retirement, she succeeded him as chairman and CEO. Under her direction, the company has continued to prosper, providing substantial income for the family and for the employees.

As Henry Williams's children grew up and began to join his real estate investing firm, he initiated regular discussions with his wife and their children. The meetings included not only those children who were joining the firm, but also the two who had chosen other careers. Their discussions were far ranging in scope, including family matters, the business and the use and distribution of the wealth. As time went on, more and more of their discussion focused on succession issues. While Henry made it clear that the final decisions would be his, family members were encouraged to ask questions and to offer suggestions regarding the process, the timing, who would be groomed to take their father's place, and the roles of each of the children who were in the business.

It soon became clear to all of them, including the oldest son, that George, the second son, was the most suited for the top spot, by virtue of the strength of his commitment, his inclinations, and his talents. Henry began working very closely with George, training him for his eventual succession to CEO, and gradually increasing his responsibilities. The family together worked out appropriate positions for the other children. Frank, the oldest son, voluntarily chose to take a position in another company, while those who stayed in the business began succeeding to responsibilities appropriate to their talents and their interests.

When Henry suddenly died, plans were well in place for the transition. There was an initial period of mourning and confusion, during which the children and other key employees were painfully getting used to functioning without Henry's leadership, talents, and energy. But before long, the organization settled down, with George holding the reins, and continued to be a successful business, serving all who were involved with it.

As Frances and Peter Anderson's children grew up and began to join the family electronics company, the parents chose to share the income with them, distributing to each a reasonably substantial portion of the company's profits each year. This decision involved considerable discussion among all of them, which helped the parents to feel confident that each of the children could be entrusted with enough income to enable them to live securely and comfortably—and that they would not use the money foolishly or lose their motivation to work.

All three second-generation members were employed in the company, in positions appropriate to their talents and interests, and they advanced into increasing responsibility and knowledge of the business. Their salaries were kept commensurate with their responsibilities, and this, together with the regular distribution of their shares of the profits, enabled them to feel reasonably secure and to live comfortably, if not lavishly.

Peter and Frances also recognized the importance of open estate planning, so that the children were not in doubt about what they would inherit—and how. Being satisfied that all the children could handle money responsibly, they left the business and the other assets to them outright, without restrictive trusts.

On the death of the parents, the children were motivated to manage the company for long-term success, without demanding excessive current income. The three worked out a way of managing it together, sharing the responsibilities of leadership according to their interests and their talents. Relationships have continued to be friendly and cooperative among them, and the business is thriving.

Power is a fact of life, by nature neither good nor bad. When misused, it usually fails to achieve its purposes, and it can damage all involved—the ones with the power and those who are subject to it. But it can be used well, so that its exercise is likely to benefit everyone—serving the family, the business and the accumulation and use of the wealth. Using power appropriately is a hallmark of maturity—of the subordination of egocentric drives to the welfare of the enterprise and of all involved. The principles that underlie the wise and effective use of power are rather clear and understandable, though not always easy to implement.

Possibly the final statement on the appropriate use of power was made some 2500 years ago by the Chinese sage, Lao Tse:

> "A leader is best
> When people barely know that he exists,
> Not so good when people obey and acclaim him,
> Worst when they despise him.
> 'Fail to honor people,
> They fail to honor you;'
> But of a good leader, who talks little,
> When his work is done, his aim fulfilled,
> They will all say, 'We did this ourselves'."

Note: The writing of this chapter was sponsored, and the copyright is held, by the International Centre for Family Enterprises (1010 Sherbrooke St. West; Suite 1610; Montreal, Quebec H3A 2R7).

CHAPTER 9
Children and Wealth
Some Questions to be Considered by
Parents and Financial Professionals

RAISING CHILDREN OF WEALTH

1. *What are important ways in which children who are, and will be, afflu-ent should be treated differently by their parents? Is it usually a good idea to provide them with things and experiences that aren't available to children who grow up in more ordinary circumstances? What sorts of limits? For instance?*

Don't give them much more than their friends and schoolmates are get-ting. Ask parents of other children what their norms are; don't necessarily believe what your children tell you about this.

Explain your limits to them, honestly. Don't tell them you can't afford what they want, if it isn't true. Setting limits provides good opportunities for discussion with children. When they want something that seems question-able, see this as an opportunity for some discussion. Look beyond a simple "Yes" or "No." Help them see why they want these things or experiences and, if possible, work toward a mutual decision.

As children mature into adulthood, many parents choose to make money available to them—in effect, an advance on their inheritance. Each parent can give up to $11,000 annually tax-free to each of their children, and, if they so choose, to the children's spouses and their children. The point here is to make money available to them when it can make a significant difference in their lives, rather than waiting until after the death of the parents, when they will probably need it less.

2. What are important issues regarding public school versus private? If the latter, residential versus day schools?

Parents must truly want what's best for their children and ensure that children understand and believe this. Here is the approach I suggest:
- Discuss issues with them; make them part of the decisions.
- Consider the quality of local public schools.
- It's often good to let them experience both—time in public and private schools.
- Some exposure to diversity—racial, economic, social, etc.—is good preparation for life.
- Choose the best school for the particular child (e.g. one with highest academic standards may be bad for a child who can't compete on that level).
- Don't send them to boarding school for the sake of the parents; children often suspect this is the real motive.
- Let them know that changing schools is always possible if they're truly not happy where they are, and the school doesn't seem right for them.

3. How much should these children be informed about the family wealth and their prospects as inheritors? At what ages should parents start telling them, and how much? What are ways of dealing with questions like "Are we rich?", "How much does Dad make?" and, "Will I be rich?"

Be sure they understand that there are no "bad" questions. These questions deserve to be taken seriously, and never treated as though the child shouldn't have asked it. All questions in this area are opportunities for useful conversations (not lectures). Find out why they're asking and what are their real questions (e.g., they may want reassurance that the family won't be in trouble). If they seem too young to get numerical answers, tell them that. Assure them that when they seem old enough, they will get whatever information they want. Treat such questions like sex: if they ask they're probably ready to know. And if they aren't asking, maybe find out why. Discuss with them what outcomes are likely if they tell their friends how much money their family has or earns. Help them to decide this is likely to have outcomes they don't want.

4. *Is it important for children to be able to earn money? If so, how do parents bring this about? How early should they be earners?*

I believe it is very important for them to earn money. They must know that if they had to support themselves, they could, and they can only know that if they've done it. The importance of the paycheck is learning that they can be paid for their work and talents. I suggest parents encourage them to get jobs, starting with work during vacations while in high school. It is better if the child finds his or her own jobs rather than the father getting one for him/her. Talk with children about the importance of work as a source of security and an essential element in the good life.

5. *Is it a good idea for parents to encourage their children to enter careers that pay well? Why or why not?*

Not necessarily. Communicate to children that work has many rewards and satisfactions, of which money is only one—and not necessarily the most important. Make clear it's their personal decision, which should not be based on what they think their parents want for them. And particularly, don't make them feel that they *should* choose their father's career, which may not be right for them. This issue is particularly crucial when family business is involved.

6. *How can parents bring up their children with a deep sense that doing creative work is an important element in living a good life? Is the best way just to require them to work by ensuring they will not be supported by family wealth, at least not until the parents die? Are there other ways of communicating the place of work in a good life?*

I suggest parents demonstrate this mainly through modeling. When children grow up in a home where parents' careers clearly provide them deep satisfaction, they'll almost certainly value creative work themselves. Also, have unpressured conversations about the place of work in a good life, and about what constitutes a good life. You can sometimes point out others who don't work and who seem to have less than satisfactory lives.

7. *How can parents help their children make career choices that will be most appropriate for them – fitting their talents and their interests?*

It is valuable to help children understand what different careers are actually like, what people *do* who choose them. Most young people have very little sense of what people in different vocations do all day. Help them to talk with people involved in careers the children may be attracted to.

Encourage vocational testing and counseling. Particularly where a child seems to have unrealistic expectations of their fitness for a particular vocation, or of the extent of their interest in that sort of work. Let them know that it's all right to change vocations; this is a benefit of inherited wealth and a reality in the modern world.

8. *What are some effective ways of preparing children for the reality that some people will be seeking ways to get some of their money? How can this be done so that they will be appropriately suspicious, without being so much so that they will damage their personal relationships and miss out on life opportunities?*

Discuss this, with parents sharing their own experiences. How have parents learned how to distinguish manipulation from sincerity? How have loans, gifts, investments, etc affected important relationships? Help them accept risk-taking as opportunities for learning. Avoid criticizing a child for having been taken advantage of; rather, just help them to see what they've learned. Help them understand, explore and accept the middle way, neither too suspicious nor too gullible. Help them learn to say "No" (or in some cases to say "Yes"). With their friends, help them consider the wisdom of sometimes making gifts instead of loans.

9. *What are some advantages and disadvantages of using parental surrogates – nannies, tutors, etc. – to help in the raising of their children?*

These relationships can be good for children, but parents must themselves spend quality time with them, and children need to feel that their parents are available. Talk with children about why they've chosen these people, and listen carefully to their feelings about them, generally and specifically. Be sure children don't believe surrogates are there because parents don't want to be with them.

10. *What are effective ways of inculcating sound and useful attitudes toward their wealth – toward using it responsibly and free of guilt?*

Mainly teach by example, by parents modeling appropriate attitudes toward their wealth. Also discussions, including talking about people they know, or know of, who seem to be handling wealth well, and those who aren't. Talk about the dangers of arrogance and shame regarding being wealthy. Always be available for discussion on this (and other topics). It is useful for parent to share their own experiences, including how they learned to be in good relationship with their wealth. It can also be useful to engage in discussions about life not being fair, and to point out that there are many forms of inherited wealth besides, and perhaps more important than, money—like intelligence, a healthy body, beauty, charm, good parenting, etc.

11. *How important is it to encourage children to become philanthropic? If it is a good idea, how can parents help bring about a sense of the value of giving and of doing it wisely and with generosity? How can they help them to become more conscious and more sophisticated in their giving?*

Encouraging philanthropy is most important. In all my experience, I keep finding that the happiest, most fulfilled inheritors are those for whom philanthropy is a significant life focus. Again, setting an example is primary, including the parents talking about their giving, their reasons, how they make choices, and the satisfactions they receive. Help them see philanthropy as a privilege, not a duty, for those with more than they need. Help them see that wise philanthropy results in the donor being grateful to the recipient, who is doing something for the donor that the donor wants to happen. And remind them that those who work in the non-profit field are usually choosing to be paid considerably less than they could earn in the corporate world. Discuss how non-profit organizations are doing essential work, which generally is not done by governments.

12. *What are some effective ways of helping children in their personal and psychological development? What about psychotherapy? Other paths?*

Therapy should almost always be encouraged, often starting with the adolescent years. It is important to see good therapy as life-enhancing, not just problem-solving. Talk about this being one of the privileges that come with wealth—the opportunity to employ skilled and wise counselors to help them through some of life's difficulties, to enhance their self-knowledge, and to lead to happier, more constructive lives.

13. *And what about their spiritual development and journeying? Is it usually a good idea to bring them into the parents' church, temple or whatever? Suppose the parents are not involved in a religious community?*

Like psychotherapy, I believe spiritual development should be encouraged as an important life-enhancing pursuit. If parents are involved in a religious community, they should discuss why and what it does for them, and make this available to the children. But children should always feel free to explore and to choose their own paths.

ESTATE PLANNING ISSUES

1. *What are some advantages and disadvantages of parents keeping their children informed about the family wealth, including their likely inheritances?*

I know of no disadvantages. I've never observed a situation where harm was done by disclosure, and I've seen many where children and families have been damaged by secrecy. Being secretive about family wealth rarely works; children usually have a pretty good idea of the extent of family wealth. Parents' being secretive sends the children the message that they're not trusted or respected. Hiding family wealth is a form of lying, and lying to one's children is almost always damaging, to them and to their relation-ship with their parents. Knowledge of the family wealth and of their prospects helps children to plan careers and life styles, as well as to become more competent at managing their assets. Informing children about family wealth and their prospects should be a periodic *discussion*, not just transmittal of information. This should include making sure that the children understand that the amounts can increase or decrease substantially. These discussions should always be done with the parents, never by the attorney or financial planner alone.

2. *Is it a good idea for parents to include their children in the process of estate planning, beyond keeping them informed factually? What's likely to happen if parents encourage children to express their own hopes, concerns, and fears regarding the process and their own inheritances? Is the resulting estate plan likely to be more or less constructive when children participate in the process?*

The estate plan is almost always better if the children are involved in the process. Parents will draw up a plan that serves everyone better if they've listened to their children and understand their needs, their wants, and their fears. In these discussions, it's essential that the parents *listen,* not just present information and talk themselves. Parents need to present the essence of their current thinking around their plan (and the plan itself, if they have already drawn one up). This presentation should include sharing their own values, beliefs, and concerns regarding wealth and their children. Then they should make clear that their plans are subject to change if these discussions persuade them that there are modifications that would be beneficial to the children. However, it should also be understood that the decisions are made by the parents, not by a democratic process.

3. If there is a family meeting where estate planning is discussed, what are the most useful and appropriate roles of the parents? The children? The children's partners?

Parents present their plan and intentions, along with their reasons. They should always be available to answer *any* questions raised by the children. And they need to listen carefully and make clear that they truly *want* to know what their children are thinking and feeling around these issues.
The children are there to learn and to express their honest opinions, hopes, and concerns. They want to know the essential elements of the current estate plan, or thinking about it, including the parents' reasons for making the plan as it is. And they should feel free to express themselves, even when this seems to risk disagreement or even disapproval from their parents or siblings. Having children's partners present is often a tricky question. Parents need to find out if their children want to include their partners (in committed relationships). If some do and some don't, then encourage the children to work this out among themselves. This issue can be especially troublesome when one of the children is in a marriage or other relationship that seem

precarious, as it can mean that others are sharing and discussing very personal matters in the presence of someone who may leave the family.

4. If a family meeting is held where parents discuss their estate planning with their children, who else should attend? Attorneys? Financial planners? Accountants? An objective facilitator?

Ordinarily it's best to have the initial meeting(s) without financial professionals so that everyone can feel maximum freedom to express their personal wishes and concerns. At a later meeting it may be a good idea to bring in the estate planning attorney, financial planner or accountant, who can provide technical information and get a better understanding of the family's wishes. Where there is an expectation of significant conflict or tension in the family meeting, an experienced, objective, professional facilitator can be of significant value. The facilitator can observe and identify existing or potential conflicts and help to resolve them. He or she can facilitate the discussion process, draw out less vocal participants, and occasionally summarize what seems to have been decided, and what are the open issues. The facilitator will ordinarily submit a written report, summarizing the decisions made, those still to be considered, and the issues remaining to be worked through. It's important that everyone involved keep in mind that such meetings are almost inevitably uncomfortable and tense. Even when relationships are optimal, these discussions center around the two biggest taboos in our culture: wealth and death, which many of us don't like to talk about.

5. If you are a financial professional and believe that children should be informed and/or included in the process, and the parents are reluctant to involve them, what should you do? Or, vice versa, what if the parents want to involve their children and you don't think it 's a good idea? How strong a position will you take here?

This depends on the nature of the relationships between the parents and the professional. The professional should at least express his/her opinion on open estate planning, citing reasons, and, where appropriate, mentioning examples (while preserving anonymity) of cases where this was or wasn't done. Where the parents don't agree with this recommendation, the professional will ordinarily drop the issue, unless and until the relationship has developed to the point where the clients seem to welcome their input when it's different from what the client believes.

6. What are some advantages and disadvantages of "incentive trusts," where heirs are rewarded financially for certain behaviors?

These are almost always a bad idea—sometimes very bad. First, there are much more effective ways for parents to transmit their values, and if this hasn't worked, bribing the children to (appear to) have adopted these values doesn't really transmit the **values**. It does encourage the children to be dishonest, to pretend to have adopted the values and behaviors that their parents prize, so as to obtain the incentives. Incentive trusts are inherently manipulative and are a rather dishonest means of controlling children. This is almost sure to be resented and to damage the relationships.

7. What about "generation-skipping trusts," where parents bequeath some of their wealth to their grandchildren? Pros and cons?

Aside from tax benefits, this also is usually a rather dubious idea. It bypasses the parents' children in what may be seen as a rather unfortunate attempt to gain their grandchildren's love and gratitude. If this kind of trust is being considered, it's essential that the older parents discuss this with their children, and they will usually be well advised to accept their children's wishes on this matter.

OTHER ISSUES

1. *What are some potential difficulties for couples where there is significant difference in wealth? What are some ways these problems can be avoided or ameliorated?*

Most of the problems associated with wealth differences are largely the result of the expectations and attitudes of others—principally the parents of the wealthier partner, but also friends, colleagues, and society generally; this is particularly true if the woman is the wealthier partner. Many parents, especially in affluent families, "know" what kind of partners their children should choose. Problems are exacerbated where there are significant educational and cultural differences, such as social skills. Conflicts around money—spending, saving, investing, and risk taking, are common in most marriages, and this can be particularly difficult where there are significant wealth differences. A man who marries a rich woman often feels inadequate when the amount of money he brings in from his work seems rather insignificant in the family. When the man is the less wealthy partner, it can be damaging to the marriage and to the children if he is seen as living off his wife's fortune and not doing his own work. Pre-martial or post-marital agreements can be stressful, particularly if they're imposed by the parents of the wealthy partner. This happens often, and is almost always a bad idea. But when they're truly agreed to by both partners, this can be helpful.

Solutions to many of the problems mentioned above are largely a matter of free and open discussion by the couple. It's very important that they get beyond the common resistance to talking about money issues and feel free to bring up their questions, and particularly their feelings, before they become too difficult. Psychotherapy—individual and/or couples—can be most helpful in dealing with their feelings and enabling them to be more open with each other around money issues. It's important that the couple, and their parents and friends, recognize that there is discomfort involved, so that they can move on through that discomfort. The young people need to try consciously not to be overly influenced by attitudes and judgments of others, particularly parents, about such marriages (again especially if the woman has the money).

2. How can people of means arrive at decisions about how much money they require? What are some of the issues they need to look at and decisions they need to make in order to arrive at satisfactory answers?

First, they need to be clear about the facts, which often means getting the help of a professional—usually a certified financial planner—in order to know just how much they have, what they're spending, and then what they can afford for various uses. Then they need to work at becoming more conscious of just how they would like to live, how much they care about optional "luxuries" like a large home (or two), automobiles, travel, etc. For a couple, this calls for rather extensive and searching discussions, particularly when, as is often the case, their desired standards of living are different. A good financial planner, attorney, accountant or psychotherapist can be helpful here, particularly by asking thoughtful questions.

Another decision, requiring searching self-exploration, is how much they wish to give to their children during and after their lifetimes. A similar decision is the place of philanthropy in their lives—how important it seems and what causes and organizations they wish to support. The self-exploration leading to these decisions can be difficult and time-consuming. It's important not to abort the process by trying to reach decisions too quickly. Many people will find in this exploration that they have acquired an attitude of "never enough," which, while largely unconscious, can seriously interfere with their making the best decisions, and with their life satisfaction.

3. What is the place of philanthropy in the lives of people whose wealth is more than they need? How do they decide on the level of their giving? How can they best choose among all the organizations and activities that could use their support?

First, in my experience, I keep finding that people of wealth, particularly if they are inheritors, who are seriously involved in philanthropy are much happier than those who aren't. Financial professionals can help people make decisions about the level of giving that makes sense for them. Philanthropic consultants and community foundations can provide information and wise counsel toward selecting the non-profits which best fit the donor's priorities. Either a family foundation or a donor-advised fund with a community foundation enables a family to make decisions together about what they wish to support. The discussions that arise in these meetings can be most helpful in assisting family members to know one another better, and in developing their appreciation for each other.

A couple needs to decide whether to give jointly or separately. Often, some of both make sense, since they're likely to have somewhat different inte-rests and priorities. Involving themselves in some of the organizations they choose to support financially – as board members, fund-raisers, volunteers, or advisors can provide great personal satisfaction as well as making their giving decisions more conscious.

4. *If a substantial amount of the wealth is in a family business, what are some pitfalls to be aware of? Specifically, what are good ways of dealing with power within the family and with succession issues?*

Again, of primary importance is open and frequent discussions among family members, around such sensitive issues as succession planning and distribution of profits. The not uncommon practice of the father (CEO) making the decisions alone, and simply announcing them, almost guarantees unhappiness and possibly serious conflict. If a family member is chosen as successor, be sure that talent and motivation are the primary criteria, not just being the oldest. And keep in mind that a daughter may well be the best choice. Under no circumstances should children be coerced into working in the family business; this is almost always harmful to the business, to the young person, and to their relationships with their parents and siblings. It's often useful to bring in outside talent, as executives and board members. Family business consultants can be most helpful, as long as they are sensitive to the relational and emotional issues involved.

CHAPTER 10
Why Me? The Inheritors' Dilemma

In all my years of consulting with those who have or will inherit significant wealth, one of the most prevalent and troubling issues I've observed has been: *Why should I receive all this wealth and its benefits, through no efforts or virtue of my own, while others, equally deserving, have to struggle for theirs?* Whether this issue is raised openly or implicitly, some common symptoms are:

• **Shame:** Feeling embarrassed at being unfairly fortunate.

• **Low self-esteem:** Believing they wouldn't be highly valued, by themselves and others, if it weren't for their affluence. Doubting that they could make it in the world without their inheritance. Feeling inferior to those who earned their fortunes

• **Getting rid of the money:** Excessive gifts and loans, bad investments, and extravagant living

• **Restricting relationships:** Limiting contacts to avoid being with the "less fortunate." Feeling that they would be judged and not accepted, or befriended primarily for their money, by those with significantly less wealth.

To some extent the inheritors' dilemma and its accompanying discomforts are inevitable. So, when this comes up, explicitly or implicitly, I often begin by pointing out that life truly does seem to be unfair, and sometimes terribly so. But I keep finding that the most effective way of helping inheritors to deal with these feelings and problems is to point out that money is just one form of inherited wealth and, perhaps surprisingly, for most of us one of the least important. Perhaps it says something about our society and its values that inherited wealth is usually seen as limited to money. Just as "What is he worth?" is assumed to mean, "How much money does he have?" However there are other forms of what should be recognized as inherited wealth, including:

- Wise and loving parents

- A fine and creative mind

- A strong and healthy body

- Athletic ability

- Physical beauty (in our culture especially for women)

- Personal charm

- A compassionate and loving heart

- Being born in a country relatively free of violence and oppression

- Artistic talents, in a variety of fields

All of these are gifts received, at least to a significant extent, with our births, though some can be enhanced and developed by our own efforts.

Few of us have inherited all of these forms of wealth, but almost everyone has received some. I then suggest to inheritors that they consider how they value each of these, compared to money.

- How would their lives be if they had inherited some of these forms of wealth that they don't believe they have?

- How would they be if they hadn't inherited those that they did receive?

- If they were able to choose, which forms of inherited wealth would they value most highly?

- Which would they relinquish for substantial money? And which do they believe most people would trade for money?

- Which of these would they give up much of their inherited fortune to acquire?

Another very effective way of diminishing the painful and debilitating effects of the "Why me?" question is substantial philanthropic involvement. Almost without exception, I keep finding that those inheritors who give significantly of their money, time, and talents to causes, organizations, and people they believe in, are the happiest and most fulfilled. "Why me?" can be answered very constructively when inheritors choose to use their wealth and their skills and efforts to contribute toward a better world, to ameliorate some of the ills that beset our planet and its inhabitants, and to enhance the quality of life for others. Living philanthropically is a privilege for inheritors, one that can alleviate the painful symptoms of the "Why me?" issue. This is particularly true when they discover causes and activities that truly arouse their passion, where they can experience enthusiasm around giving back some of what they were given.

I also encourage inheritors to cultivate a practice of gratitude, being aware and appreciative of their own good fortune. Recognizing and appreciating what we've received enhances the quality of our lives and helps us to keep perspective on our good fortune. Consequently, those who pursue the practice of gratitude help to free themselves from some of the potentially unfortunate consequences of being an inheritor.

To summarize, when inheritors accept that life is unfair, recognize that money is only one form of inherited wealth, use their money and their time philanthropically, and are grateful for what's been given them, they can most effectively counter the painful and destructive consequences of the "Why me?" question.

CHAPTER 11
Can Inheritors Save the World?

This chapter explores the idea that those who have received, or will inherit, significant fortunes can make very meaningful contributions toward improving our world. Because of their wealth, of course, inheritors are uniquely situated to make a positive difference. But there are other resources, described below, that can empower them to have a significant beneficial impact. Not incidentally, the use of their resources, time, energy and contacts can be very rewarding to them, enhancing the quality of their lives. These are the reasons I want to encourage affluent parents—and their children—to develop attitudes and to take actions that support making this larger contribution with their wealth and their lives. What I'm proposing here is also of value to leaders of foundations and non-profit organizations dedicated to improving our world.

I am writing, in part, because of my own experience of inheriting a significant amount at a rather early age. This enabled me to leave my job and devote myself to working with, and giving money to, several non-profit organizations. For me, this involved people and groups who were spiritually and psychologically oriented in their efforts toward improving our world. This involvement has been so rewarding to me that I continued in this kind of work after I ran through enough of my inheritance that I needed to earn money again.

This is not exactly a new idea, of course. We know, or know of, individuals and families who exemplify this, who devote much of their lives and their fortunes toward making our world a better place. The Rockefellers are perhaps the most prominent and best known as a family with a tradition for generations being guided largely by the principles of generosity and service.

Inheritors of substantial wealth can become conscious, responsible, and wise philanthropists, studying non-profit organizations devoted to causes they believe in to learn which of these seem to be the best qualified to fulfill their purposes. Their involvement can be not only financial but also personal, by volunteering their service on boards or in other capacities. They may devote very significant time and energy to such service, a form of philanthropy that can be as valuable, to the recipient and to the donor, as money. And they can use their contacts with other affluent people in fundraising for these organizations.

Giving generously of time, talents and money is likely to bring about very desirable changes in our world—such as easing suffering, solving some of society's pervasive social and economic problems, reducing conflict, encouraging the arts, supporting education at various levels, and preserving natural resources and treasures. Worthy and beneficial as these endeavors are, they mostly don't qualify as "saving the world," as advertised in the title of this chapter. But there are causes, organizations and people that, with adequate support, could bring about the transformative changes needed to avert the disasters that seem to be confronting us—such threats as climate change, resource depletion, and major wars that could involve nuclear, chemical and biological weaponry.

To achieve these sorts of changes, philanthropists need to focus their wealth and their efforts on the *root causes* of these problems, not just their *symptoms*. These root causes are the attitudes, decisions and events that give rise to and are ultimately responsible for the difficulties and problems confronting us. They include such attitudes as greed, arrogance, self-centeredness, unchangeable opinions and judgments, lack of compassion, excessive materialism, competitiveness, and short-sightedness. Because our country is so powerful, the most significant and potentially destructive of these mind states are those of the American people and our leaders. There are a number of fine organizations dedicated to dealing with these root causes and, naturally, all are dependent on infusions of money and of the time and talents of staff and volunteers.

Inheritors can bring to philanthropy addressing root causes, not only their money but also other unique personal gifts. They can study economics, finance, politics, current events, ecology, psychology, spiritual disciplines, and related fields, toward preparing themselves to use knowledge and wisdom in their compassionate work. Through their families and their social connections they can influence other people of means toward having a similar focus in their lives, not just the merely wealthy but people who also have very significant power and influence. If they don't have full-time occupations, they will have the time and energy to learn about, and devote themselves to, causes and organizations they believe in. And they can learn, work and interact with like-minded inheritors in such groups as the *Doughnuts, More Than Money*, and *Changemakers* that provide information, ideas, support and companionship to their participants. *Responsible Wealth* is a rather recently formed organization of people with wealth in the upper 5 percent of the U.S. population, working within and outside of the political arena toward making our economic system more fair and equitable.

Helping their children toward this life emphasis provides a significant and joyful opportunity for wealthy parents. Through their personal examples and their teaching, they can raise children for whom serving humanity is the highest value. They can make clear that earning money is not necessarily a life-enhancing goal for those who will be wealthy in any event. They need to inform their children what their inheritance prospects are, to enable them to plan their education and their lives knowing to what extent they will need to devote themselves to making money and how much of their time and wealth they can give to philanthropic pursuits. Parents can distribute some of their wealth to their children before their own deaths, helping them to learn first-hand how to manage their money and how best to give it, and enabling them to devote time and talents to non-profits. They can educate them about philanthropy, both through their own knowledge and by bringing in authorities. And, very importantly, they can allow the children to make their own mistakes, such as choosing non-profits that turn out not to be the best, and then let them know that they welcome these mistakes as valuable learning opportunities.

What inheritors gain from devoting much of their time, energy, and wealth to causes they believe in is truly wonderful. Most of us who have done this have found great satisfaction in our involvement with organizations, causes, and people to which we can respond with enthusiasm. We learn a lot and we feel blessed in aligning our efforts and talents with our convictions. We generally find that the people who devote themselves to this work—as staff, volunteers and board members—are those we find most congenial and admirable, people we want to spend time with. This sort of involvement goes far in decreasing the guilt and shame experienced by many inheritors for receiving wealth they haven't earned and feel they don't deserve. And they usually experience enthusiasm and delight in these activities, feelings often notably absent in working for money they don't really need. Such involvement can bring true richness to lives which otherwise seem rather bland, boring, and meaningless. In my work and my friendships with inheritors, I've found that those with a philanthropic center are generally the happiest and most fulfilled.

To summarize: Inheritors, with appropriate parenting, can make a very significant contribution toward a better world for all of us and for future generations while greatly enhancing the quality of their own lives. And I believe that there is potential here for a truly significant *movement* as more people of privilege shift their priorities and their efforts to doing what they can to improve our world and to forestall potential disasters.

(This chapter was suggested and significant ideas offered by Oleg Gorelik, CFP)

CHAPTER 12
Wealth and Spirituality

This chapter explores the relationships between wealth ownership and spiritual awareness and practice. I hope that it can help wealthy people and their advisors to understand how a spiritual attitude and practice can enhance the possession and the use of wealth and how being affluent can help in the pursuit of a more spiritually based life.

I am writing this, in part, because of how important the relationship between wealth and spirituality has been in my own life, as well as those I have known and consulted with. I've learned that people whose wealth brings them true happiness tend to have a spiritual orientation toward it that involves seeing it not just as my wealth, but as a *gift* to be used wisely and with a generous spirit.

Let me begin with what I mean by spirituality, a word difficult to describe and that has different meanings for each of us. To me, spirituality represents an attitude of awe, reverence and searching, inspired by the recognition that there is a great deal beyond our physical beings and environment. With that attitude has come a commitment to pursue this conviction and to make it an increasingly central element in my life. For many of us, spirituality provides not only enhanced meaning but also a pervading sense of well-being and happiness. We can't be spiritual because we're told to be or because we feel we should be; we have to want to follow this path. Of course, we also have to recognize that some people who are quite spiritually oriented don't use the word as a self-description, and some who use the word easily don't actually seem to be following the practice. To me, "religion" involves affiliation with a group or institution whereas "spirituality" does not require involvement with institutions, although it may.

I believe it is helpful to introduce this topic by describing something of my own spiritual journey and how it has affected my attitude toward wealth. To summarize, my inheritance provided me with the time and opportunities to pursue a spiritual path, and my growing spiritual awareness made my wealth truly a gift.

I was blessed with wise and caring parents, but religion and spirituality had no meaning for me until I attended a three-week "Sequoia Seminar" in the mid-1940s led by a Stanford professor and his wife, Harry and Emilia Rathbun. This seminar was focused on the teachings of Jesus, not necessarily as "the truth" but because his teachings helped us to look at core questions in our lives and to use the answers we discovered to live more deeply satisfying lives. After years of struggle, I realized that I wanted a life lived meaningfully and that there were visions and principles to guide us along the way.

Following a 10-year career in the construction business with the Bechtel Corporation, in the mid-1950s I inherited enough money so that I left and began working with the Sequoia Seminar for a half-dozen years, helping in administration and leading seminars and discussion groups. While there I became acquainted with, and for eight years volunteered with the American Friends Service Committee. There I learned much about spiritually oriented service and how meaningful it is to those who serve. Exploring the Quaker teachings, and eventually joining a Friends' Meeting, I pursued my spiritual journey and experienced its rewards. Also, around this time, I became involved in the early stages of the Esalen Institute where truly innovative approaches to psychological awareness and spiritual development were being explored. Their offerings provided me with another important learning experience.

Building on what we had learned in a half-dozen years with Sequoia Seminar, a group of us started "San Francisco Venture" in the early 1960's—a personal growth center that included social service work in a ghetto neighborhood. With good fortune, this led me in the mid-1960s to become the executive of the newly formed "Association for Humanistic Psychology." This being the 60's, AHP quickly became a very popular and innovative organization that spawned the "Association for Transpersonal Psychology" and its companion Journal. This organization brought psychology and spirituality together beautifully and connected me with a wonderful community of inspiring mentors and fellow journeyers, some of whom are still friends and colleagues. These experiences helped me to learn a great deal about how I could use my management experience and talents to further what I truly honored.

Because I hadn't had a paying job in the twenty years since leaving Bechtel, I was beginning to run out of money. So, in 1977 I was delighted to accept the paid position as Executive Officer of the C.G. Jung Institute of San Francisco. This work over more than a decade, accompanied by my Jungian analysis, helped me greatly in developing my psycho-spiritual consciousness and in continuing to make meaningful contributions with my life.

The Jung Institute position was part-time, and I soon discovered that I needed to earn more. I then realized that my experience had prepared me for a career that I began in 1980 as a consultant on inherited wealth, working with parents, inheritors and families on the personal issues inherent in major inheritance. Again, this provided me with opportunities to be helpful to people and to promote spiritual values like generosity, compassion, integrity and openness, as well as to learn much on the way.

During the early 1990's I also served for three years as assistant to the President of the *California Institute of Integral Studies,* a graduate school that integrates psychological and spiritual perspectives, eastern and western teachings, and the professional and the personal aspects of life. Here again I was privileged to associate with and learn from a number of fine and knowledgeable people.

These many threads in my spiritual seeking eventually led me to Buddhism, which is now my chosen path. Meditation, in various forms, is central to my life these days. No truly spiritual practice is easy, but I've found the effort and inevitable discomfort well worth the price.

With this as background, let me describe some of the important ways in which spirituality can affect our relationship with wealth:

• How we **receive** our wealth: A "spiritual attitude" can be a powerful antidote to offset the experience of many inheritors who receive wealth as a burden or with feelings of shame, low self-esteem, and doubt for people's motives for liking them. One of the "Eight-fold Paths" of Buddhism is "Right Livelihood," which means earning our living in ways that benefit rather than harm others and our world.

• How we **invest** our wealth: Many spiritually oriented people invest their funds in companies that treat their employees well, make products that benefit and do not hurt people, and that don't damage the environment or contribute to global warming.

• How we **use and enjoy** our wealth: A spiritual awareness brings with it a tendency toward moderation in our spending and a concern for its effects on others and the earth. We look beyond what our wealth will do for us and tend to enjoy its benefits responsibly and with appreciation for the experiences it allows and with gratitude for the gifts it brings.

• How we **transmit** our wealth: Estate planning from a spiritual orientation is often a process involving the whole family, not just the parents, and is done with a heightened consciousness of the effects of the distributions on the recipients. Affluent parents with this orientation tend to avoid giving their heirs a sense of entitlement and encourage them to find their own goals and ways, without an expectation that they be "successful" or "should" be exactly like their parents. The trusts drawn up by wealthy families with a spiritual orientation tend to include a sizable proportion for non-profit organizations that promote and reflect the values of the donors.

• How we bring **meaning** to our lives with wealth: A spiritual consciousness tends to bring with it new priorities in living that go far beyond material success, pleasure seeking, and impressing others. Instead, we often look for ways to make a real contribution to the world and, in our philanthropy, it inspires attitudes and practices of generosity.

• How we approach **philanthropy**: A major discovery of a spiritual path is that true giving rewards the donor at least as much as it does the recipient, whether it involves giving our money, time, or attention. Spiritual teachings make clear that giving out of a sense of duty, of what's expected, to impress others, or in any spirit but that of heartfelt benevolence, is not true generosity and is not deeply rewarding. My own experience over the years, as well as those of friends and clients, makes it clear that those who are generous with their money and their time, giving to organizations and causes which reflect their deepest values as well as to individuals, are significantly happier and more appreciative of their lives than those who choose otherwise.

A spiritually oriented life benefits all who choose it, but in some ways especially the affluent, by giving us the freedom to make choices regarding our lifestyles, relationships, child-rearing, vocations, and avocations. This freedom of choice can enable us to make decisions that reflect our deepest values and to look beyond the materialism that our culture and media tend to hold out as "the good life." Being affluent can be of considerable value in developing our spiritual attitudes and practice. We can afford psychother-apy, spiritually oriented workshops, retreats and seminars, psycho-spiritual advisors/guides, time for reading, meditating, and travel to inspiring places and teachers.

Still, money does not automatically bring happiness. A friend recently visited Bhutan and told me how people live in this spiritually oriented culture. There are few really wealthy people, mansions, or fancy automobi-les. Instead, informed by a long history of spiritual practice, the Bhutanese people emphasize sharing resources, supporting family relationships, and integrating spiritual practice and ethics into everyday life. Various global studies on happiness during the last few years have rated Bhutanese among the happiest people on the planet—far beyond Americans.

Some religions teach that being wealthy brings its own dangers. Jesus is reported to have said: "It is easier for a camel to go through the eye of a needle than for a rich man to enter into the kingdom of God." This is some-times interpreted as meaning that being wealthy is "bad" or "unhealthy." I believe, rather, that this teaching is intended to call our attention to the dangers confronting the wealthy. When we overly value the possession of wealth and admire others simply because they have a lot of money, we have indeed lost our way. Truly spiritual values and living lead us to view wealth as just another fact of life, neither to be worshiped nor despised. Once we accept that life isn't fair, we can commit ourselves to doing what we can to offset this and make a difference.

My life experience has helped me to better understand the relationships between wealth and spirituality and how they can enhance one another. My inheritance made many rewarding experiences possible and enabled me to associate with friends and mentors who personified the spiritual attitudes and orientation that I have been seeking. Wealth also made it possible for me to follow my heart's desire to keep finding meaning in life and work and to share this with others. I am deeply grateful that these opportunities, activities, and relationships have brought me freedom from boredom and a continuing enthusiasm for working and living. It is my hope that others may also find their connection between money and spirituality equally fulfilling.

CHAPTER 13
You Can't Take it With You: Preparing for Death

An essential part of the aging process is preparing for dying and death. Unfortunately, many of us are in varying degrees of denial that these are ever going to happen to us. In fact, various studies have shown that over half of American adults do not have a will or other estate plan and, surprisingly, the percentage of wealthy people without such documents is even higher than the average.

Given our culture of denial, the purpose of this chapter is to encourage readers to face the reality of death and to make the preparations that will best serve them, and those they leave behind. These preparations include the practical as well as the psychological and spiritual aspects of dying. The information and ideas I am presenting here are drawn primarily from my own experience, and my own preparations, particularly over the past few years. Some practical reasons for making these preparations include:

• To insure that distributions from your estate are as you want them to be. For those who die without appropriate documentation of their intentions, the state will usually step in and, by default, dictate how the estate will be distributed.

• To minimize problems for survivors. Out of consideration for emotionally distraught survivors, it is helpful to those who will have to make decisions and take actions regarding your belongings and their distribution.

• To improve the quality of your life and to bring peace of mind, it is helpful to have made essential preparations.

• To determine whether you have enough assets to support you through the probable rest of your life and, if not, to take whatever steps you can to deal with this challenge.

In reviewing preparations, probably our most important, practical task is ensuring that we have in place appropriate legal instructions for the distribution of our assets to the beneficiaries we choose. Often this consists of a "Revocable Living Trust," which is usually preferable to a will alone, because it doesn't require probate, as wills do in most states. This trust specifies distributions of your estate to the beneficiaries you choose, as well as names the trustee(s) and successor trustees (in case the named trustee cannot carry out these duties). It is very important to discuss this with the trustees chosen, so that it's clear that they're willing to take on these responsibilities. In many cases attorneys and other professionals handle the work under supervision by the trustee.

The trust can specify whatever distributions you wish, including cash, securities and personal property, instructing the trustee(s) to carry out these wishes. In almost all cases I strongly recommend that this document be drawn up, or at least reviewed, by an attorney. Where the estate or its distribution is complex, or where there is any likelihood of controversy among heirs, you should choose a lawyer who specializes in estate planning.

Your "Living Trust" doesn't include funds in your retirement account. Distribution of these on your death is specified in "Beneficiary Forms" provided by the funds in which your retirement accounts are invested, and for each of these you need to specify your primary beneficiary and contingent beneficiaries, those who will inherit your retirement funds if your primary beneficiary(ies) are not living. Distributions from your retirement accounts to your spouse are not treated as taxable income to him or her until they are withdrawn. Distributions to anyone else are taxed as their income when they are received, so most people make their spouses the primary beneficiary of their retirement accounts.

Both your Living Trust and your Retirement Account Beneficiary forms should be reviewed every year or so to ensure that they still reflect your wishes, and revised as necessary. I and others with whom I have worked, often find ourselves confronting resistance to looking at all this again, and we need motivation and self-discipline to face this rather daunting task regularly.

I've known a number of families, especially those with significant wealth, who have held one or more meetings of all concerned family members to discuss distribution of their estate. You may want to begin by telling them, perhaps in writing, the essential elements of your current estate plan, making clear that you welcome their input and are open to making changes if this seems right. If your estate is large and/or complex, you should instruct your estate-planning attorney to provide a rather brief summary of its provisions, in plain, easily understood English. Where there is likely to be conflict within the group, many families have brought in an outside mediator/consultant to help with this process to insure that everyone there is heard. This is a role I've taken with a number of wealthy families, and I've learned that the presence of a neutral facilitator can increase the comfort of those involved and help them to be more open and honest with one another.

Where applicable, your Living Trust should specify those you have named to take responsibility for your children who are minors. Of course, you need to discuss this with these people to be sure they will accept these responsibilities. You certainly need to discuss this decision with your children, if and when they're old enough.

Where the funds to be passed on are quite significant, and/or if you have strong philanthropic inclinations, there are a number of kinds of *charitable trusts* and/or *bequests* you can choose. You set up these trusts with the advice of a planned giving specialist or estate planning attorney who can counsel you about which form of trust is most useful in your situation. Philanthropic trusts can offer significant savings in income and estate taxes, especially for large estates. If you do this, it's important that your heirs know about it, understand your reasons, and how this will affect their inheritances. A good option for many, especially if the amount to be given is not very large, is a "Donor Advised Fund"—available from community foundations and some other organizations. For a relatively modest fee, they handle all the paper work and have staff that is knowledgeable about non-profit organizations. Whether it's a charitable trust or a donor advised fund, it's often a good idea to have the giving decisions made by the family, including adult children. This not only empowers the young people but as they discuss their giving interests, it helps them to know each other better.

PREPARING A MESSAGE TO YOUR SURVIVORS

One of the ways you can better prepare for your own death is to write a message to your survivors that lays out in detail your instructions, wishes, and information about where to find certain documents. This can be a very valuable gift to your survivors. Although this may not be an easy task to accomplish I, and many other people I have known and worked with, have found it a most gratifying experience and achievement. To do this I suggest you imagine yourself in the place of your survivors and jot down all the things that they would need to do once you have died. Here are some suggestions for what to include:

INTRODUCTION

• Begin the message by saying why you are creating this letter; its importance to you and your survivors, and that you will be updating it from time-to-time.

• Address the letter to everyone you want included.

• State the importance of distributing it in advance in order to allow for questions and discussion and possibly revisions.

YOUR ESTATE

• Describe where to find important papers: the Living Trust (which some of them should already have), recent tax returns, insurance documents, professional papers, important personal correspondence, etc. Instruct or make suggestions for what to do with some of these, which should be distributed and how, destroyed or shredded, etc.

• List the names and contact information for your attorney, financial managers, accountant, and so forth.

• If you have a safe deposit box, describe its location, where the key is kept, what is in the box, and who you have authorized to open it.

• Write out instructions for how to distribute your possessions—home, furnishings, automobile(s), art objects, clothing, music and video, photographs, etc. Indicate who you want to receive certain objects, especially those with significant monetry or emotional value, suggest how to make decisions on others, what to do with those none of them wants. In doing this, it's important to keep in mind perceived fairness, to avoid dissension and disappointment.

You may want to let your survivors know the *very approximate* value of your estate now while you are alive, with strongly stressed caveats about how this may change, especially if you need to spend much for your own or others' illnesses. Indicate briefly how your *Trust* distributes these now, with explanations as appropriate. And, if you would like, make it clear that any of this can be changed and that you are inviting their input, questions, and suggestions. You may want to set up a meeting of all involved to discuss all this, particularly if this is something they would like. In my professional experience I've learned that there should be **no** surprises when an estate plan is implemented; these often lead to disappointments, resentment toward the dead person and conflict among heirs.

OFFICE CONTENTS

• Include where to find significant items such as checkbooks, credit card information, tax returns, and other important papers. List papers, records, etc. with instructions on what to do with them, what to keep, discard, distribute, etc., and what is confidential and should be destroyed.

• Describe any valuable office equipment such as a computer and how to dispose of these.

PERSONAL PROPERTY

• Create a brief summary of valuable belongings, books, art, furnishings, etc. and how you would like them distributed or disposed of. Identify particularly valuable items and perhaps specify how to distribute them. Indicate your preferred method of decision making regarding who gets what. Suggest what is to be given to Goodwill, the Salvation Army, and so on.

• List personal correspondence, diaries, records, etc., and what to save and what to discard.

• Mention your will/revocable trust. Make sure all who should know about this have copies or essential summaries and/or know where to find them. If you are open to discussing these you can state that in the letter.

There are very useful pamphlets available from several hospice organizations that give information on these and other issues. I suggest you contact a hospice in your area to learn about these issues, and to possibly discuss them with their staff.

PREPARING FOR THE END OF LIFE

An important part of your letter to survivors will be communicating your desires for the last phase of your life. To do this you will need to reflect on what you want this to be and where you want to die. I recommend that, if feasible, this not be in a hospital, since the medical responsibilities usually interfere with the atmosphere we are likely to want at the time of death. To consider our own death, also means that we need to grapple with the psychological and spiritual issues that may arise from our fears, concerns and unfinished business. You may find it helpful to speak with a close friend or family member or see a therapist to help you work with any issues that arise when considering the dying process. By taking the time to process our feelings and consider our options we can:

• Ameliorate the anxiety and depression that almost always accompany the realization that death is coming.

• Make the dying experience optimal for ourselves, those close to us, and our caretakers.

• Be helpful and supportive to others who are dying.

• Feel more ease with whatever we may experience after our death.

Completing and distributing the following documents can help make clear our wishes:

• Instructions for Health Care: Enables you to state your wishes about medical care when you can no longer speak for yourself. This makes specific your intentions regarding treatment when your death is imminent and medical care can only prolong your life, often rather briefly, or when your consciousness is such that continuing to live seems not worthwhile.

• Power of Attorney for Health Care: This names someone(s) to make decisions for your medical care when you are no longer able to do so. It supplements the Instructions described above.

• Donations of Organs at Death: States your wishes regarding organ donation. This task is optional; the prior two definitely should be prepared.

These documents must be witnessed by two people and/or a notary public to be operative. In your letter consider including how you want to be cared for when you can no longer care for yourself:

• Describe your wishes and whom you would like to make the decisions about where you will live—nursing home, live-in care, etc.

• If you have a Long Term care insurance policy, describe it and say where to find papers.

Also include in your letter your wishes regarding the dying process:

• Who will be in charge and make decisions. Also, specify backup(s).

• How you want to die, where, with whom present. Specify if you want to have hospice care.

• Describe the spiritual surroundings and support you want. Including if you want spiritual guidance such as a spiritual counselor, clergy, or other. Would you like special photographs or artwork present or special music playing? Are there especially meaningful writings you would like to be read to you? What else?

• How and to what extent you wish to avoid being a burden for spouse, children, and others.

• Include copies of the above documents including the Durable Power of

Attorney for Health Care, with your instructions about what extent you wish to be kept alive in terminal state. Be sure to update as you age.

• Express your wishes as to funeral arrangements, disposition of your remains, and memorial service.

• Disposition of the body. What are your wishes for burial, cremation, etc? Your wishes for a memorial, funeral or other services. Also whether you want a newspaper obituary.

• Death Certificates. Who you would like to take responsibility for this.

COMPLETING YOUR LETTER

Consider including the following:

• An invitation to your survivors to provide suggestions for changes and additions.

• I urge you to finish this letter with sincere expressions of your affection for and appreciation of those you're leaving behind. This can mean a lot to them both now and later, and I suggest you'll find the experience of writing these words most rewarding.

I encourage you to review this letter fairly often, as you're likely to find you want to make some changes, and then distribute the revised letter to those involved. I've done this every year or so, and, by the way, it's a lot easier to revise this than it was to write it the first time.

The information stated above comes from a very valuable document, called "Advance Healthcare Directive," prepared and distributed by *Compassion and Choices*, a fine non-profit organization focused on enabling people to die as they wish. You can download all these materials from their website, **www.compassionandchoices.org** or write them at: PO Box 101810, Denver, CO 80250-1810. The requirements for these forms vary from state to state, so you'll need to indicate which state you want the information for.

For the process of dying, a good deal of information and counsel is available in books, articles, videos, etc. Some books that I and others I know have found especially meaningful in preparing for this experience include:

- *The Ultimate Journey: Consciousness and the Mystery of Death*, by Stanislav Grof.

- *The Grace in Dying: A Message of Hope, Comfort, and Spiritual Transformation*, by Kathleen Dowling Singh.

- *Who Dies?: An Investigation of Conscious Living and Conscious Dying*, by Stephen Levine.

- *Advice on Dying: And Living a Better Life*, by the Dalai Lama.

- *The Tibetan Book of Living and Dying*, by Sogyal Rinpoche.

- *Graceful Passages: A Companion for Living and Dying*, an audio CD by Gary Malkin and Michael Stillwater.

There are many other fine books in various spiritual traditions.

Hospice organizations have been developing and growing all over the country. Their staff and volunteers are there for terminally ill people and their families, and those I know of are wonderfully helpful and supportive. Besides being present for the dying person, they are trained to be there for those being left behind, during and after the dying process. They offer advice and instructions for caring for the dying person as well as emotional support for those dealing with the expectation and the actuality of the loved one's death. Their compassionate support can also be helpful to family members preparing themselves for their own deaths and reducing anxiety.

Hospice workers can provide assistance with the physical aspects of dying, including palliative measures to reduce physical pain. And some hospices focus on the spiritual aspects of the dying process—which can be very helpful. I encourage you to learn about the services and assistance that your local hospice provides.

This chapter is based on my own experience and research. I've tried to cover the issues but I know that as you look into this, you'll find other information and resources. My principal, heartfelt message is "Don't put it off." Death really is going to come to you and those you love. The more you're able to accept it and consider and implement appropriate preparations, the better your life and those close to you is likely to be.

APPENDIX A
Facilitating Family Meetings

The primary purpose of the meetings described here is the development or modification of estate plans. Typically, the meeting will involve only family members—parents and children—who are directly affected by estate plans. The spouses of the children may or may not participate, depending on the wishes of the parents and all the children. Sometimes financial professionals—estate planners, accountants, financial planners, and investment managers—will be included as consultants to be called on for their expertise, not as active participants.

As a facilitator I usually begin by asking the participants to say something about how they're feeling now, what they're hoping for from this meeting, any apprehensions they're aware of, what they want from other members, and anything else they want to add. I suggest that these need to be rather brief statements, given the work we have to do, but that it's important to all of us that they say what they want the group to know about them.

I often ask the parents to let the family group know what their current estate plans are, making it clear that these are subject to change as a result of this meeting. I will propose that this be done beforehand, in writing and distributed to all participants.

Then we develop an agenda that I record on a blackboard or flip chart. I write down all the topics that participants propose for discussion, and then arrange them in some sort of reasonable order. I make it clear that this is not a rigid agenda, and that any participant can always raise other items.

We then go through this agenda with my guidance and facilitation. When appropriate, or when asked, I will add my own observations and opinions, but this is usually a minimal part of the discussions.

One of my most important functions in these sessions to insure that everyone has adequate opportunities to speak, and, most importantly, that *they are heard.* When it seems as though some members are dominating the discussion, I will bring this up and remind them that everyone needs opportunities to speak. And if I sense that someone's statements are not truly being heard, for whatever reasons, I will bring this up, often by asking the person if they feel their statement has been truly listened to.

When it seems as though an item has been adequately discussed, I will suggest that it's time to move on to the next one and ask the group if they agree. If not, we will continue with the item that doesn't seem completed. I will have the agenda in mind and how much we need to cover in the time we have. If we seem to be running behind, I'll suggest that we either need to move faster or to set a time for another meeting.

Whenever conflict seems to be arising among family members, I'll suggest that we stop what we're doing and see what can be done to resolve it. If there's general agreement, I'll take the role of mediator and help them to become clearer about what the conflict is about, the kinds of feelings and thoughts that are present, and how to resolve it, at least well enough so that we can proceed with our discussion.

After we've finished talking about the items on the agenda, I'll ask participants if they have any further questions or items to discuss, or if they have any statements or questions they want to direct to the parents or to others in the group.

When desired, I write up a summary of decisions reached and plans made. I may add my own observations about the family with suggestions about what they may want to work on, individually and together.

APPENDIX B
Peacemaking: The Resolution of Conflict

Most of us live with a fair amount of interpersonal conflict, largely because we really don't believe that it can be resolved. And most of us find ways to avoid bringing it out into the open, fearful of fantasized results and the anticipated unpleasantness of dealing with disagreeable feelings and expressions—both our own and that of our adversaries. Whether expressed or not, controversy within families—within and between generations is a common experience. This is particularly true where money is involved. Marriage counselors find that disagreements over money are by far the most common source of conflict within relationships. But family conflict is often not necessary—it usually can be resolved, or at least reduced in intensity.

We often devote considerable energy to conflict—usually in an adversarial mode. We want to keep the battle going in order to win. But, with rare exceptions, resolving matters amicably, and becoming free of the antagonism and mistrust, would be much more to our advantage. And, if we search within ourselves a bit, we usually find that this is what we really want.

For the past twenty-five years, I have been helping families with interpersonal antagonisms and misunderstandings. This has been a significant part of my professional work as a consultant to individuals and families on issues related to the inheritance of wealth. Disagreements, resentments and mistrust—between and within generations—are likely to occur even in the most congenial families. I have seen the damage—both short and long-term—that such frictions can engender. Dissension often interferes with the achievement of family goals and enterprises—financial and otherwise. Particularly if it isn't expressed openly, conflicts inevitably interfere with relationships and closeness within the family.

I have found, over and over, that such strife can be resolved or significantly reduced. And this can often be achieved rather easily. For example, one family with which I worked had battled for several years over issues having to do with the transmission of wealth. Relationships were strained, and communication was scant and often distorted. But, when they decided to try to change this situation, two days of meetings resulted in resolving the issues to everyone's satisfaction, and relationships have since become quite harmonious. There are still disagreements over some issues, but the participants find they can live with these and that such differences need not get in the way of their relationships. For such resolution to happen, there are certain preconditions:

• The adversaries must really *want resolution*—want the war to end. This can be trickier than it seems, since people sometimes have a personal, emotional stake in keeping a conflict alive. It is helpful for participants to ask themselves what they may believe they are gaining by maintaining the dissension. Do they really want to get along better with their adversary?

• Participants need to be *reasonably confident* that the situation can be improved. Whether or not they believe that this is possible usually serves as a self-fulfilling prophecy.

• "Combatants" must be *prepared to risk* being candid with each other. This means revealing their feelings—anger, anxiety, resentment, mistrust, fears, hopelessness, or whatever. It helps to be aware that the anticipated risks often turn out to be unreal—that expressing what they have been holding back does not necessarily bring painful results—often just the reverse.

• Each party must be willing to allow the others to express their own feelings, and to hear and accept those feelings. For this to work, participants *commit themselves to listening*. Really hearing another person, especially when strong feelings are involved, is considerably more difficult than it may seem.

• Each participant needs to be ready to consider that he or she *may be wrong* on some matters, and then be willing to change his or her mind. When this happens, they must be willing to tell the others about this change.

Wherever there is the possibility of strong antagonism, or where the stakes are high, it is usually wise to bring in an experienced, skilled, and objective facilitator. Such a person can help to keep the conversation focused, to ensure that each has ample opportunities to speak, and that they hear each other. Also, the presence of a facilitator makes the parties feel safer and more willing to take risks. There are many qualities that are desirable in a good facilitator; an essential one is that all parties to the conflict trust him or her. The facilitator may occasionally *suggest* a compromise solution, for consideration by all parties, but will never attempt to *impose* an answer. The facilitator is a mediator, not a judge or an arbitrator.

Given that the participants really want to reach constructive resolution and are willing to accept the risks—real and imagined—that this can entail, what can they do now? Many techniques have been developed for helping people to work through their conflicts, but they generally share these elements:

• The parties to the conflict *come together* with a mutual, stated commitment to work toward resolving their difficulties. This means that they agree to stay together, in one or more meetings, for a long enough period to give the process a fair try. In making this commitment, the parties must be aware that the situation may get worse before it can get better. Opening up conflict can elicit and expose strong feelings, and it takes some faith to trust that the situation will turn around, and that, if they continue there will almost certainly be a diminution of antagonism, mistrust, and fear. *The commitment to seeing it through is crucial* because aborting the process of resolution can worsen the situation.

• They *express to each other* their willingness to be as candid as they are able to be about their thoughts and feelings—not only those from the past, but particularly what is happening in them in the moment. It helps to start the meeting with expressions from each of the parties about their current feelings.

• In indicating their *intention to listen* to the extent of their ability, they each give permission, in advance, for the other party to question whether he or she is really being heard. It's hard to overemphasize how powerful real listening can be in resolving interpersonal strife.

• They agree to minimize the rehashing of past offenses and injuries, since this is usually unproductive, and often counterproductive. Instead, they attempt to keep the conversation current by dealing with present reality, invoking the past only when it seems necessary for understanding the present.

Where there is a mutually shared desire and commitment to deal constructively with conflicts, and where the participants agree to do their best to adhere to the conditions described above, I know of no situation where significant resolution has not taken place.

To sum up, conflict is normal, between family members and with people in the family office. Most families tend to ignore such conflict, because they really don't believe that resolution is possible. But experience shows, repeatedly, that when people really want to eliminate or reduce such friction and dissension, it can be done.

APPENDIX C
The Perils of Family Money

This piece, written by Lisa Gubernick, was part of a larger article, titled "The Perils of Family Money," that appeared in *Forbes Magazine* in June 19, 1995.

But for a $300,000 inheritance, John Levy, now 73, probably would have remained a construction executive. If the money had not run out, he probably would not have become a pioneer in the new profession of wealth counseling. Levy, great-grandson of the co-founder of Alaska Commercial Co., a trading company, got an engineering degree at Stanford, then spent ten years rising rapidly at Bechtel Corp. When he was 33, his father died, and the inheritance, which was equivalent to 1.5 million in today's dollars, landed in his lap. Levy quit Bechtel to work, unpaid at the Sequoia Seminar, a Christian counseling service. Twenty years later, the money ran out. He had no interest in returning to the construction business, so Levy got a job as executive director of the C.J. Jung Institute of San Francisco, a training center for analysts. There he met Frederick Crocker Whitman, an heir of California railroad baron Charles Crocker. Whitman had done his own research on the potentially debilitating effects of wealth, coining the word "affluenza." He figured that Levy could advance his research. "I discovered [psychological] literature on the subject was virtually non-existent," says Levy. "There was shelf after shelf on sex, but no thing about money." Levy devoted five years to the study, interviewing scores of heirs, parents, and therapists.

Conclusions: The expectation of a substantial inheritance can often result in delayed maturation. Levy contends that "too many [heirs] are like the butterfly which never develops if it gets outside help in the process of breaking out of its cocoon." Parents, no matter how wealthy they might be, must make sure their children work. "It's the only way that children will develop self-esteem, by learning they can survive on their own". Levy has worked (at $250 an hour) with a hundred affluent families as a counselor over the last 15 years. Chicago's Harris Bank has used him to help run the seminars for its wealthy clients. The Stranahan clan, who sold Champion Spark Plugs for $280 million in 1988, hired him to help them sort out how to handle their money. Since Levy got started, a mini-industry of wealth counselors has sprung up.

About John L. Levy and His Consulting

After graduating from Stanford with a BA in Engineering and an MBA in the late 1940s, I spent ten years in heavy construction as an engineer and executive with the Bechtel Corporation. Then I received an inheritance that enabled me to spend the rest of my professional career in non-profit organizations devoted to psychological and spiritual issues, first as a volunteer and later, in paid positions, as my inheritance was spent. I've served in managerial positions, provided personal counseling, and facilitated group interactions. Organizations for which I've worked include: Sequoia Seminar, the American Friends Service Committee, San Francisco Venture, the Association for Humanistic Psychology (as Executive Officer), the C.G. Jung Institute of San Francisco (as Executive Director), and the California Institute of Integral Studies (as Interim Provost).

For the past 25 years I've had a private practice working with individuals and families on issues involving inherited wealth. I've made presentations and led discussions for financial planners, estate planning attorneys, family office managers, bank trust officers, investment advisors, and other professionals throughout the U.S. I've also written a number of articles on topics related to inherited wealth; most of which were adapted for this book.

The primary consulting services I offer are:

• *Helping affluent parents and children identify their needs and wishes in the inheritance process and to become more conscious of their concerns, hopes, and fears.*

• *Counseling inheritors, parents, and family groups around their issues related to the transfer of wealth. A central element in this is the preparation of inheritors to live fulfilling and rewarding lives.*

• *Facilitating intergenerational discussion of estate planning and other sensitive, and often tension filled, issues. Sometimes this involves mediating troublesome conflicts within and between generations.*

• *Assisting individuals and families to clarify their philanthropic aims and choices.*

While I do share some of my own experience and thoughts with clients, my primary consulting objective is to help them to discover and clarify their own priorities and to implement them in their lives. My own experience as an inheritor, confirmed by my observations, research, and consulting over the last 25 years, has convinced me that the inheritance experience need not be a negative one, but rather can be one that has exciting and fulfilling potentials. My work with wealthy individuals and families is based on this conviction.

SOME UNSOLICITED COMMENTS FROM MY CLIENTS

"….the time you spent with our family group was extremely productive, and provocative. I say provocative because you helped us challenge many of our long-held assumptions about how we should think, act, and how we should raise our children. Thank you again for your work, and for the gentle, yet professional way you facilitated our discussions."

"I've been wanting to thank you again for the extraordinary help you offered the family. Your acute sensitivity to each of us combined with your mastery at holding the reins lightly (but holding them nevertheless!) created the ideal framework within which each could express himself freely (as never before!). You were wonderful!"

"You said a lot about management of family assets, communication, "control", and much, much more. But you also made us think and feel about the importance of things not so tangible and measurable."

"I want to keep thanking you! You were so emphatically the right person at the right time for me. It made all the difference."

"We regard our (family) meeting to have been the most successful we have ever had, due in no small part to the knowledge and tone which you brought to our discussions."

"What a wonderful experience last week! Everyone, as you know, felt this family meeting was the best ever. Your centered presence was just the ingredient—people clearly felt safe, respected and carefully facilitated."

"I am grateful to be able to trust working with you. My shame around money is definitely diminishing."

"I want to proclaim your complete success in the family meetings last week. You led the way with masterful sensitivity, and you brought loving healing to a family which had been in painful disarray."

"I can't thank you enough for your help and brilliant counsel and caring involvement over the months that augurs well for a "new beginning" between (my daughter) and me. As a result of our meeting, in the best possible atmosphere, I am relieved and happy."

"You clearly are a master at dealing with the complexities of family relationships, and I know that we all emerged form the experience with a new sense of our directions and relationships with one another."

"Remarkable healing and growth took place that weekend, and your participation was crucial."

Made in the USA
Lexington, KY
22 March 2012